ANXIETY AND PANIC

Self-help solution, therapies and cure suggestions to panic attacks. Depression and phobia workbook for relief and rebalance. Stress and anger management in relationships and children.

Table of Contents

Introduction 1

Chapter 1 The Truth About Anxiety And Panic Attacks 6

Chapter 2 New Techniques To Deal With Anxiety And Stop Panic Attacks 16

Chapter 3 Who Gets A Panic Attack? 36

Chapter 4 Grateful & Perspective 49

Chapter 5 Meditation 56

Chapter 6 Increasing Your Self-Awareness 61

Chapter 7 Meditation And Mindfulness 69

Chapter 8 How To Get Rid Of Unpleasant Memories With EMDR 77

Chapter 9 Common Difficulties In Using The EMDR Method 84

Chapter 10 "8 Simple Exercises" 88

Chapter 11 Improving Ineffective Communication Skills 99

Chapter 12 Find Your Core Issues 116

Chapter 13 Emotional Relief 134

Conclusion 153

Introduction

The human body has a set of instincts that ensure its integrity and survival. For example, reactions - to run, fight, hide, freeze, shrink and so on. These instincts are automatically activated in situations dangerous to humans. Unlike animals, people are able to suppress their instincts due to higher nervous activity, that is, intellectual control. If the conflict between instincts and intellect takes a lingering nature, this leads to the fact that a person ceases to "hear" the body. He completely suppresses his instincts and begins to live by one intellect.

Such a split between the body and the intellect is very characteristic of people suffering from manifestations of anxiety and fear. They are separated from their bodily sensations, cease to feel the body and "go to the head." Such people try to live by intellect and logic alone; they cannot rely on their instincts and intuition, because both instincts and intuition are closely connected with bodily feeling. Such people lack natural grace and spontaneity; they are used to deciding with their head what the body should do and how it should feel.

And if, reading these lines, you realized that you are just such a person "disconnected from the body", then your first priority should be the following: make friends with your body and return to your natural instincts and again learn to "listen" to it.

Sometimes such a split between the head and body occurs as a result of a shock injury. A shock trauma is a situation when a person's life or physical integrity is in danger, and events develop so quickly that not one of the instincts can help him. For example, during an accident, what is happening is so fast that a person does not have time to adequately respond. At this moment, all of his survival instincts are activated immediately, but not one of them can lead to any completed action. A person cannot escape or hide in such a situation. And as a result, he just freezes in confusion.

This condition is also called stupor. A person physically freezes in one position, because at the same time many opposite aspirations act in him - to run and hide, fight and pretend to be dead. Figuratively speaking, the human nervous system simultaneously presses both the brake and the gas. In an extreme situation, his body immediately activates all its survival programs - in the hope that at least something will work. But this only leads to the fact that a person just freezes in place and motionlessly watches what is happening.

When a person realizes that pain or death is inevitable, he has only one opportunity to adequately respond to this situation - to withdraw from the body.

He ceases to feel the body and thus tries to avoid pain and destruction. Some people describe this condition as follows: "The soul went into heels." Or they say: "It was as if I jumped out of the body and watched everything that was happening from the side, and at the same time I did not feel the body." Indeed, in a state of shock, a person does not feel pain; therefore, such a reaction of dissociation of bodily sensations in itself is also adaptive and helps him survive. But the problem is that often a person is "stuck" in this reaction. And a long time later, even after all the bones have already grown together and the wounds have healed, a person continues to be afraid of "being in his body". He is more comfortable in keeping body sensations at a distance.

People, who have experienced sexual abuse, act in a very similar way. "Being in the body" is too painful for them, it causes unpleasant associations and memories, and also activates the anxiety and fear that they once experienced.

The body for man is also the greatest gift, and carries the greatest danger. Only the body is capable of experiencing pleasure and truly enjoying life, but on the other hand, it can also be a source of pain. The body is perishable, subject to destruction - that is why the intellect has learned to separate itself from it, in order to get the illusion of its safety and security.

Separating himself from the body, a person loses the ability to be "alive" and spontaneous, experiencing sincere joy and other emotions, but acquires a sense of security. And very often people choose this security.

But such a departure from the body does not solve all the problems. The bodily sensations, squeezed out of consciousness, often return in the form of neurotic symptoms - anxiety, chronic clamps and stresses, headaches and psychosomatic diseases. The extreme degree of dissociation of the body causes feelings of derealization and depersonalization. Therefore, working with the body is an integral part of restoring the psycho-emotional balance.

Chapter 1
The Truth About Anxiety And Panic Attacks

You might already suspect that you have an anxiety disorder. It's a normal process that happens to everyone. For example, before giving presentations, or going into interviews, most will experience an elevated heart and breathing rate and feel a bit nervous. That's a completely natural and common feeling and just your body getting you ready to face something important or intense. When this feeling goes even further, on the other hand, starts rising in intensity, and making you feel nauseous, lightheaded, or uncomfortable, that's when it becomes a problem. A disorder occurs when you have powerful, frequent anxious episodes that end up getting in the way of you functioning in life.

Different Anxiety Disorders to Know about:

There are actually a few different types of this issue that you should be aware of. The more knowledge you have about yourself and your condition, the better you can find the treatment that will help you. Here are the different types of anxiety disorder:

Generalized: The first type of anxiety disorder is GAD, or generalized anxiety disorder. This is the presence of excessive panic or anxiety for no known cause or reason. According to research from the ADAA (Anxiety and Depression Association), this problem impacts 6.8 million adults every year in the United States. This issue may be diagnosed when this state of anxiety persists for at least half a year. In severe cases, sufferers have a hard time holding a job, or sometimes even leaving the house. In milder cases, however, it's possible to lead a more typical life.

Social Anxiety: This is a bit more specific than generalized anxiety disorder and includes fear about social environments or situations, including being humiliated or judged by other people. This phobia ends up making sufferers feel alone and ashamed, often times, and it affects roughly 15 million U.S. citizens according to ADAA research. It typically comes on around age 13, and 36 percent of social anxiety disorder patients end up waiting more than 10 years to seek help.

OCD (Obsessive-Compulsive Disorder): Some people don't know that OCD is considered an anxiety disorder, as well. People who suffer from this feel a compulsion to perform specific tasks or rituals repeatedly. This can include checking on something, obsessive organization, counting, or washing your hands very often. Someone with this ailment typically doesn't feel okay until they can perform this task.

PTSD (Post-Traumatic Stress Disorder): This can develop once someone has experienced or witnessed something very difficult, violent, or traumatic. They often relive something painful repeatedly, and might be withdrawn emotionally, get angry fast, or have outbursts. The symptoms of PTSD might start right away or could come on years after the incident or incidents. Physical attack, natural disasters, and war are all common triggers of PTSD, and anxious episodes can come on with no signs or warnings.

Panic Disorders: this results in panic attacks, spontaneous anxiety, impending doom, or terror. This might lead to shortness of breath, pain in the chest, or heart palpitations, and these attacks might come on at any moment regardless of the situation. When someone has an anxiety disorder, panic attacks are often a part of it. This can cause someone to isolate himself or herself, feel ashamed, or withdraw from others.

Phobias: These are also classed as anxiety disorders. Phobias include fear of heights, spiders, or small spaces and create a strong urge to stay away from the situation or objects that are feared. In some cases, a phobia is just an aversion to something, while in others, a phobia can become a sort of obsession that interferes with normal functioning.

Perhaps your anxiety encompasses more than one of these categories, which is quite common. Regardless of how bad your anxiety is, there is hope for you and the simple methods in this book will help you gain control back over your own mind and life. Before continuing with tips and methods for this, let's look a bit deeper into different anxiety symptoms.

Symptoms of Anxiety Disorders:

Anxiety might occur in a variety of ways and the symptoms could be unique to the sufferer or the specific type of disorder. However, all anxiety disorders include intense concern or worry about a specific subject for over half a year. Let's look at some other general symptoms of anxiety disorders:

Restlessness: Sufferers of anxiety often find it hard to calm down or relax, even when they are not in a physically threatening situation. This results in irritability and nervousness, along with difficulty paying attention or concentrating. You might find it impossible to listen to those who are talking to you because the thoughts in your mind seem so loud and overwhelming, which is normal for anxiety sufferers.

Insomnia: It can be really difficult to fall asleep when you're anxious, and some sufferers even wake up in the middle of the night with their heart racing and pounding. This trouble sleeping results in fatigue due to not getting enough rest regularly. This can cause you to start doing poorly in work or school, which then further fuels your anxiety, causing a self-defeating, negative cycle.

Other Physical Symptoms: In extremely anxious states of mind or panic attacks, the sufferer might experience weakness or trembling, dizziness, along with difficulty breathing, sweating, feeling too hot or cold, and tingling or numbness in the limbs or hands. They might feel pain in the chest and start hyperventilating in extreme cases.

Consequences of not Dealing with your Anxiety:

Everyone knows that intense anxiety doesn't feel good, but it can have a host of other consequences. A persistent or excessive anxious state leads to harmful effects on your mental life and physical health. Let's look at some of the complications that can result from not working on getting your anxiety under control.

Short-Term Effects: When you get anxious, a flight or fight response happens in your body, releasing hormones and chemicals, such as adrenaline, into the body. This causes your breathing rate and pulse to rise to give more oxygen flow to your brain, allowing you to respond quicker to serious or life-threatening situations. This might even give your body's immunity a short boost, and once the stressful stimulus passes, your body can go back to normal.

A Weakened Immune System: But if you feel stressed and anxious on a regular basis, and it lasts for extended periods, you can't ever recover or return to normal because your body never gets the needed signals to calm down. This leads to a weakened immune system and a higher risk of sickness and viral infections. Stress on a prolonged basis can lead to overall ill health and bad physical conditions.

Digestive System Effects: In addition to anxiety affecting your immune system over time, your digestive and excretory systems can also suffer an impact. Harvard Medical conducted some studies and found that IBS (irritable bowel syndrome) could be related to anxiety disorders.

Lower Libido and Appetite: Anxiety disorders often result in a loss of libido and appetite. It can also result in headaches and serious muscle tension and discomfort over time. When someone has panic attacks regularly, they might start to actually fear anxiety, fueling the cycle even further. Being in a constant panicked or stressed state like this often leads to depression and a lack of energy, and heightens risks for heart disease, diabetes, and blood pressure problems.

Who is at Risk for Developing this?

Anxiety disorders occur at all ages and life stages, but they most commonly begin to set in around middle age. In addition to this, women are far more likely to develop anxiety disorders (by 60 percent, according to research). Of course, going through stressful experiences increases the risk that you will develop this kind of disorder, but symptoms might appear to be unrelated since they can set in years down the road. Abusing substances or having other medical issues can eventually result in anxiety problems, as well.

Recognizing the Signs:

Even after having experiences with anxiety and reading this chapter, you might still have doubts about whether you have an anxiety disorder or not. Of course, the best way to know for sure is to consult a medical professional, but it also helps to look for some signs. It can be hard to pinpoint this type of disorder, especially if they exist in tandem with drug abuse, physical sickness, or other mental disorders. Here are some signs of anxiety disorder to keep an eye out for, both in yourself and loved ones:

Social withdrawal and fear of going outside of your home.

Unwarranted and extreme fear towards harmless things or situations.

Personality changes, either suddenly or over time.

Repetitive or compulsive actions and behaviors.

Issues in school or at work, on a repeated basis.

Suicidal or depressed thoughts on a regular basis.

Physical and emotional issues happening often.

What to do about Anxiety Disorder:

For anyone who recognizes such symptoms in themselves, seeking professional help is important, but that's far from all you can do to fix this problem. In fact, there's a lot you can start working on, right now, to help assuage this problem. That is what we're going to cover in the following chapters of this book. To begin with, you first have to realize and believe that you can change for the better. You learned how to be anxious, therefore you can teach yourself not to be.

Chapter 2
New Techniques To Deal With Anxiety And Stop Panic Attacks

For the average person, paying attention to their precise feelings and sensations can be somewhat challenging. It's simply down to the fact that there's too much noise—both internally and externally. Most people are helpless against negative emotions, anger, and anxieties—but through a mental training exercise known as mindfulness meditation, or simply mindfulness, one can finally perceive their emotions, thoughts, and sensations in their purest form.

The following are some of the benefits of practicing mindfulness meditation.

Relieves Stress

Mindfulness alleviates stress. By incorporating the mindfulness exercises, one is able to rid themselves of the symptoms of stress. Many studies have backed up the idea that mindfulness is a powerful method of fighting away stress. For instance, parents who are into mindfulness meditation can easily overcome the stress induced by kids, veterans who have unstable moods can overcome their stress-inducing thoughts, and workers become more grounded once they get into mindfulness. Mindfulness increases a person's capacity not just to alleviate stress but to avoid it in the first place. If one is into a regular practice of mindfulness, their mental health is going to be in perfect condition.

Increases Inner Peace

Without inner peace, we forbid ourselves from becoming the best, and our potential goes to waste. But through mindfulness, we are able to elevate our minds and spirits and attain inner peace. When we are at peace with ourselves, we are attuned with our talents and desires and are inclined to achieve success when we apply ourselves. Inner peace is critical for the development of a person in both the individual context and in their wider role of serving the society. After all, if a person was conflicted, they'd make terrible friends, schoolmates, life-partners, employees, employers, and even leaders.

Alleviates Anxiety

Anxiety is the scourge of modern society. The staggering sales figures generated from anxiety-suppressing pills are a testament to this fact. But anxiety limits a person's capacity to express their needs and function within society. Thankfully, there are mindfulness exercises which can be taken up in order to relieve a person of the anxieties. But in order to achieve results, the person must transform the exercises into a routine. When anxiety is gone, a person ceases to have a frenetic mind and becomes more high-energy. With the end of anxiety, a person becomes more inspired, and their level of focus goes up.

Improves Sleep Quality

If you have been getting too much or little sleep or none at all, your quality of life has no doubt suffered. You have probably become cynical, hostile, and short-tempered. Poor sleeping habits can do serious harm to a person's life. But through mindfulness, you can improve the quality of your sleep, and by extension, your life. There are various mindfulness exercises to help a person acquire great sleep. There's even scientific evidence to support this fact. Some senior citizens who reported sleep disturbances were exposed to mindfulness, and in as short a time as one week, they had recovered fully.

Improves People's Capacity to Withstand Illnesses

Mindfulness may not exactly get rid of the symptoms of an illness, but it replenishes the sufferer's mental and emotional health. If an ill person maintains a positive attitude, their chances of a full recovery are pretty high, unlike the ones who have lost hope and are bitter. There are various mindfulness exercises that help ill people boost their positive energy. Research into people suffering from terminal illnesses such as cancer who have undergone mindfulness training shows an incredibly positive outcome; patience experiences less fatigue, improve their spirituality, and become motivated.

Improves General Health

You don't have to have life challenges of any kind in order to get into mindfulness meditation. You can get into it for the sake of improving your overall health. Mindfulness cultivates behaviors that promote perfect health, such as routine health checkups, being physically active, and avoiding drug and substance abuse. Mindfulness also heightens your spiritual awareness. This is a major factor in developing your gut instincts and capacity to make the right decisions.

Considering that the long-term success of an individual is, to a great extent, an aggregation of all their decisions, mindfulness plays a great role in pushing them toward success, particularly by heightening their intuitive capabilities.

Supports Weight Loss

In a world where unhealthy eating is the norm, obesity has graduated into a crisis. Nowadays, obesity is not the reserve of old people who have had enough time to consume all the fattening foods the world has to offer, but even young kids are becoming obese. Many overweight people are looking for a solution to their problem. Thankfully, mindfulness is a less taxing solution than say, lifting weights. Mindfulness helps people fight off their tendency to eat while stressed out and promotes weight-loss through cultivating healthy eating habits. Additionally, mindfulness helps people commit to habits that will keep their weight in check, for instance, working out.

Improves Attention

Another benefit of mindfulness is the fact that it helps in boosting attention. Many people have reported that their attentiveness always receives a boost from engaging in mindfulness meditation. Other benefits touch upon memory, executive functioning, and visual-spatial processing.

Fights Loneliness

Another reality of the modern world is loneliness. Maybe you are alone by choice or through circumstances. But you don't have to be lonely. Through mindfulness, you can boost your mental energy, safeguard yourself against energy vampires, and live without any shred of loneliness. Senior citizens are more vulnerable to loneliness than any other demography, and they stand to benefit greatly by adopting mindfulness meditation.

Defying Age

A person who meditates regularly is no stranger to the statement, "You don't look your age!" Meditation helps them look younger than they really are. And then people who meditate tend to live far longer than average people. It's no secret that people are superficial. People judge you by your looks. But then an individual that meditates is likely to be in great shape and also have healthy skin.

Improves Brain Health

One of the benefits of meditation is the fact that it boosts brain health. When your brain is functioning at an optimum level, you have a sharp focus, and it helps you advance much quicker. Researchers found out that people who meditate on a regular basis tend to upgrade about nine regions of their brain, which results in the following benefits:

Improved cognition

Decreased stress

Increased happiness

Quality sleep

Improved learning

Improved memory

Higher EQ and IQ

Willpower

There are so many people out there who have "potential," but sadly they get overwhelmed by reality and end up dropping out of the race. In a sense, these people lack willpower. The world is a tough battleground, and it takes someone with a fighting spirit to achieve their goals. Willpower is the act of hanging on even when you should be discouraged, trusting that you have something of worth, and never yielding until you get your way. It is an extremely important skill for survival in the modern world. Willpower goes together with mental stability. Meditation improves an individual's mental health; in that sense, meditation equips an individual with the ability to be persistent in their quest for success.

Creativity

No matter what area you can think of, there'll always be a need for creativity. Creativity never goes out of style. The awesome thing is that people are naturally creative. However, most of that creative energy has been buried under negative emotions, distractions, and inactivity. People who meditate on the regular tend to have higher creative energy. This boosts their competency when compared against non-practitioners. Creativity always stands out, and it's more often than not rewarded.

Intuition

Intuition is the ability to comprehend a certain scenario even without looking at the facts or evidence. It's also called gut feeling. Sometimes, our intuition may contradict our rational mind, and in a world that puts a lot of emphasis on being rational, intuition gets a bad rap. But amazingly, ultra-successful people have confessed to using intuition more than their minds, when making key decisions. Steve Jobs, the founder of Apple Inc., once said, "Intuition is more important than intellect." Warren Buffett relies on his intuition when buying out a company. And even Bill Gates uses his intuition to make key decisions. Of course, this is no encouragement to use intuition at the expense of your mind. You should strike a perfect balance.

The benefits of meditation are endless. But most people seem to have a misconception about meditation. There are no barriers to practicing meditation. You can perform in any serene environment. Some people think that meditation is a light exercise, and of course, they are mistaken. If done the right way, meditation is an extremely taxing exercise, and this is because it consumes a huge amount of mental resources.

A seemingly simple meditation exercise involves the following steps:

Step One: Being Comfortable

You start off by assuming a comfortable position. You can be sitting, standing, or lying on a bed. You basically assume a position that feels most comfortable. Comfort is necessary as it will allow you to assemble together the focus needed to practice meditation.

Step Two: Close Your Eyes

Can you meditate without closing your eyes? Of course, yes—but when you close your eyes, you get to raise your concentration and improve the experience. In fact, you can even put on an eye mask to achieve your aim.

Step Three: Do Breathe

At this point, you now have to focus on your breath. Let it be natural. As you focus on the inhalation and exhalation process, pay attention also to how other parts of your body respond. Place your hand at different parts of your body and pay attention to how you are feeling. Finally, you may start observing your thoughts. Some of them will be positive, and others will be negative. You will have an urge to fight the negative thoughts, but you must not do it. Just take the role of an observer and watch your thoughts pass across your mind.

TYPES OF MEDITATION

Mantra Meditation

As the name implies, this type of meditation is about repeating a word or phrase, a mantra, in order to achieve a certain goal. The mantra meditation is most effective during periods of emotionally-charged events. For instance, if you are engaging in a competitive sport, and it is the finals, you can practice mantra meditation in order to get into a winning mindset. Also, if you are sorrowful, you can practice mantra meditation in order to overcome the grief and be happy again.

Walking Meditation

Some people are not into "still meditations." The biggest reason is anxiety. Also, some people have a strenuous schedule, which means they haven't the time to sit still and meditate. Such people have an alternative choice in walking meditation. The walking meditation, as the name implies, is practiced when an individual is walking. As they consciously put one step in front of the other, preferably down a quiet road, they may inhale and exhale carefully, while watching their thoughts. If they are walking down a noisy road, they can plug in earpieces and take a listen to soothing music. Walking meditation combines both spiritual and physical aspects to raise the individual into a higher plane of wellbeing.

Mindfulness Meditation

In this form of meditation, one is brought back to their present. So many times, we are distracted and held back from completing our immediate goal. For instance, if we are at a restaurant having a meal, we might get distracted by other things or people near us. This keeps us from enjoying our meal. Mindfulness meditation is particularly used for restoring your senses to the current moment. In the case above, you start by shutting down your peripheral vision and turning on your tunnel vision. This is to simply stop watching the world from the corners of your eye and turn your full attention to the food before you. And then next you have to focus on the sensations that the food elicits. Pay attention to the texture of the food against your tongue, the taste, and the aroma. This will allow you to savor your food at a much deeper level.

Loving-Kindness Meditation

This type of meditation is practiced in order to boost positive emotions within us or to send them out towards a particular person or thing. This type of meditation is beneficial during hardships, either at a personal level or about someone you care about. You start by assuming a comfortable position, preferably sitting cross-legged on the floor, and then close your eyes, and start calling to your mind positive energies. If a negative thought crosses your mind, fight it away. Let feelings of joy, happiness, merry enter your mind—and try your best to visualize people having fun. Soak in that energy.

Spicing Up Your Meditation

The term "meditation" may conjure up the image of a clean-shaven man assuming the signature yoga-stance in a quiet, illuminated, white-walled room. There's nothing wrong with it. Meditation can be used to achieve various goals. But the great thing about mindfulness meditation is that it empowers us to tap into our creativity, for as long as we observe the ground rules. The following are some of the creative ways that mindfulness may be practiced:

Meditation Near a Campfire

There's something surreal about meditating while the tongues of fire dance right in front of you. This type of meditation appeals to people who want to turn their lives around. Maybe you have not attained the life that you'd aspired to, and it depresses your spirit, or maybe you have finally decided to confront your fears. Fears can be manifest in a number of obvious and not-so-obvious ways. For instance, if you have been struggling with the fear of rejection, you might have been a somewhat anti-social person, hiding under the guise of "wanting to be alone" when you were really afraid of getting rejected. But staying away from people means that you have missed out on opportunities for building both your career and personal life. This is the motivation you needed to take the bold step of confronting your fears.

Build the campfire so that it burns bright under the dark sky and take a few steps back to ensure that you're within safety radius. Sit down with your legs crossed at your ankles and open your hands. Then, shut your eyes. The bright flames should illuminate your face.

Take a deep breath, and as you breathe out, let go of your tensions. Take another deep breath, and as you breathe out again, stretch your upper-body. Then, take another gulp of air and hold still. Get into a relaxed state. As the air escapes your mouth ever so slowly, start watching your thoughts.

Observe your negative thoughts through your mind's eye, but instead of letting them fade away, borrow from the fire in front of you and ignite these thoughts. If you're struggling with fear of rejection, figuratively set it alight, and watch it burn into ashes. Ensure that you set all of your fears alight.

You're only to stop when all of your fears and negative bodies of energy have been set ablaze. Toward the end, your mind should seem like a blank template, at which point you should call on your imaginative powers and envision the campfire. Open your eyes.

Meditation During a Rainstorm

When the strong gusts of wind come calling, and the heavy rain starts falling, the last thing on our minds is to be cool about it. We want to dash and hide from harm's way. A rainstorm seems to terrify nearly every one of us. But what most people fail to realize is that a rainstorm has an incredible cathartic appeal. The dark clouds, heavy rain, and strong winds make for a great recipe of washing away our pain. The strong tapping of the rain is particularly helpful in calling on the unhelpful thoughts to the fore.

For those who cannot stand in the rain for medical reasons, you may meditate from a window overlooking the skies, or your balcony. But you stand to benefit most if you can actually feel the rain.

First off, you have to be in the right attire, typically light clothes, so that they will get glued to your skin under the sky. As the magnificent tapping of rainfall roars out there, hold your door open and step out into the rain. Slowly, start walking in a linear direction, with your head bowed, and your clothes fast becoming wet.

As you walk along, start calling to mind all the painful experiences you have endured. These painful thoughts should surface on your mind, with the rain acting as a catalyst, as one chaotic and jumbled dance of thoughts and noises. Depending on the severity of your pain, you might find yourself wanting to howl through the rain, which is perfectly okay.

Let the rain soak you wet, and don't try to hold back the terrible thoughts. Your mind will go through an intense phase of unraveling all your painful thoughts. Start imagining the rain, washing away your pain. Let your worries, pains, fears get carried away by the waters of the heavens. As you progress through your meditation, the painful memories and thoughts are continuously going to become less potent, eventually ceasing. Stand at attention and lift your eyes to the heavens, let the rain cleanse you. Then, walk back to your house, slowly, in a reflective mood.

Meditation Near Flowing Water

Flowing water heightens the power of meditation by calming the mind and inducing a feeling of non-attachment and lightness. If you're not in a location that graces you with naturally flowing water like a stream or river, you can have the artificial sounds of flowing water playing on your record, in a serene setting. Ideally, you should be in a setting with a natural body of flowing water.

If it's a lake, just come near the banks, but if it's a stream or a river, or an ocean, it's okay to dip your feet into the water.

As the gentle waves crash into your legs, you will feel a light sensation overwhelm your body. Focus on savoring your thoughts and energies. Notice your thoughts as they pass through your mind, but don't fight against them. Just take on the role of the observer. Let the gentle waters fill you up with light, unburden you, and make you positive.

Meditation Near a Waterfall

The beauty of life is in the wide range of things that happen to us. One moment, we are happy—and the next moment, we are grieving. When our hearts are broken, it can be easy to lie to ourselves that we are going to be okay, when we clearly won't. Suppressing our pain is akin to slowly baking a bomb of emotions that will eventually go off and ruin our mental balance.

Sitting safely and comfortably near a waterfall and listening to its beautiful melodies is a great way of practicing mindfulness meditation. Close your eyes and call on your thoughts, watching them as they drift, and then imagine the beautiful waterfall surging through your mind, cleansing your impure thoughts. Through focused intention, watch the waterfall carry away your pain, frustrations, and worries. Finally, open your eyes, wash your face from the waterfall, and walk off quietly.

Chapter 3
Who Gets A Panic Attack?

According to research, there is evidence that points out over 6 million people in America suffer panic attacks and disorders all of which are classified as anxiety disorders. In fact, according to reports by the Anxiety and Depression Association of America (ADAA), between 2-3% of Americans experience a panic attack annually, and this is common among female gender as compared to the male. Panic attacks typically affect people more in their 20's but are often seen in children, older adults and among adolescents.

The cause of a panic disorder is not well understood, but what is known by researchers is that panic attacks are not hereditary and hence cannot be passed down in families through the generations. However, it is common among people who are already suffering from other forms of anxiety disorders.

For instance; someone with obsessive-compulsive disorder (OCD) is highly likely to experience a panic attack especially when their schedule is interrupted. Additionally, people who struggle with a phobia of any kind are said to be susceptible to panic attacks. E.g., someone with acrophobia may have a panic attack in a penthouse. On the other hand, someone with a generalized anxiety disorder, a condition that is characterized by worry, often experiences constant anxiety that has been showing to escalate to panic attacks. Also, people with PTSD have a higher chance of developing a panic attack as compared to the general population.

Steps to Overcoming Anxiety and Panic Attack?

In literature, you will find so many ways that have been highlighted to play a role in overcoming anxiety and a panic attack. Most of them are not practical at all and do not help in the long-run. However, one of the surest paths you can follow to overcome anxiety and a panic attack is to be able to train yourself to respond to such situations in a calm and collected manner. And the only way in which you can be calm about it is if you accept the situation in the first place.

In this section, I would like you to reflect carefully on how these steps compare to what you do when you experience a panic attack. The truth is, the panic trick often makes us believe that our gut feeling on how to respond to anxiety and a panic attack is to do something that worsens the situation instead of making it better. Trust me; if you intend to overcome anxiety and panic attacks, you have to be willing to do things outside your norm. This is because, by doing things the same way each time, chances are you will reap the same old outcomes over and over again.

With these five steps, you can effectively guide your response when experiencing a panic attack. If you use these steps regularly, you will begin to achieve your goals at overcoming anxiety and panic attacks. These five steps include:

Step 1: Acknowledge and accept

You have to bear in mind that all forms of progress begin at this point. This is one of the most important steps in overcoming anxiety and panic attacks. You have to begin by acknowledging your current reality that you are afraid and are beginning to panic. Do not try to ignore it or even pretend that you are not anxious. Many people think that by distracting themselves from the whole situation, they might stop thinking about it and snap out of it instantly. Acknowledging does not mean that you are in danger.

Do not allow your mind into thinking that you are in danger, lest you begin to panic.

Now that you acknowledge your current reality, it is high time that you accept that you are afraid. Don't fight that feeling, rather ask God to help you take it away. Simply accept it like it were a cold or a slight headache. When you have a slight headache or a cold, you don't bang yourself on the wall, do you? Why? Possibly because it makes the whole situation worse. Understand that overcoming panic begins with you working with and not against the anxiety and panic symptoms.

You may be wondering 'but how can I accept anxiety and panic?' the truth is, even though panic attacks feel awful, it is not harmful! Being anxious will not kill you or make you crazy. Panicking and having someone pointing a gun at you are not the same things. This is because the latter might get you killed. If someone starts pointing a gun at you, the first reflex would be to run, hide, yell, negotiate, beg or fight back.

Alternatively, if a police officer gives you a parking ticket, you can live with that and what you can do at that point is to keep your temper in check so that you don't make matters worse for yourself. Simply accept the symptoms and do not resist. Ask yourself 'what can a panic attack do to me?' it can make you afraid, and anyway, that is the point of the attack in the first place, right? Therefore, if you are experiencing an attack, you are already in it. In other words, you are already experiencing the worst that could happen, and nothing can make the situation worse than it already is. All you need to do is ride it out.

But why should you accept the attack? Simple; because the more you tend to resist, the worse the panic gets. In other words, when you develop a habit of accepting the situation as it already is, the more progress you will make towards achieving your goals.

Step 2: Wait, Watch and Work

Wait

Once you have acknowledged and accepted the reality, the next thing is for you to wait, watch and then work. By "wait," it means that you are not supposed to do something other than stand there. You could choose to count 1 through to 10 before you can get mad. Understand that the hallmark of anxiety and experiencing a panic attack is the fact that it robs you of the ability to think logically.

The best thing that you can do is to think, recall and focus. It is this step that will simply buy you more time to regain your senses before you do anything stupid that you might regret later. If you are like many people I know, you will likely run away or struggle. In other words, you end up doing things that make the situation even worse.

When you jump into action so fast, you are making it hard to overcome anxiety and panic. Therefore, even though you may feel an urge to leave or make a rush decision, do not convince yourself that you cannot leave. It is better to keep that option open for when you need it to get out of the trap. The point is, stay in the situation rather than run away to get relief. Instead, allow relief to come to you.

Watch

The main reason why this step is important is just so that you can observe how panic works. You can do this by making a panic diary or journal wherein you can write down all your thoughts and experiences to help you take note of all the important elements of a panic attack. This way, you are able to respond effectively to the whole situation.

Many people say that when they fill out a panic diary, they feel the worry slowly go away and they can keep their cool. You may be thinking 'how does that work?' Well, the truth is that they are not distracted from the subject; they are simply distant from the emotion. It works well because while you try to fill out your diary, you assume the role of an observer rather than a victim.

Don't write in your diary after the attack; do it during the attack. However, if at that particular moment and setting writing won't be practical, then you can choose to use a digital recorder. If there is someone close to you, have them read out the questions to you and then record your responses. If you are driving, you can also choose to pull over for just a few minutes to write.

Work

If you are in a passive situation when experiencing a panic attack, wait and watch is all that you need to overcome your anxiety. However, if you are in a more active role like driving, then you can use this step of work. This is by simply remaining engaged in your activity.

Step 3: Action

This is a very critical role in overcoming a panic attack by simply making yourself more comfortable. At this point, you have already mastered the two most important steps; step 1 and 2. Here, what you need to ask yourself is what are you doing during the attack? The truth is, many times, people think that they can bring the attack to an end.

However, understand that it is not your job to bring the attack to an end. It will happen irrespective of what you do. Well, don't take my word for it, the best thing that you can do is to review your experience with panic attacks and ask yourself whether you have had any that did not come to an end.

The catch is for you to learn to respond to anxiety and panic in the most compelling manner. The point is for you to bring that attack to a soft landing and eventually it will end. However, if you try too hard to struggle and resist it, trust me, you will not only make matters worse, but the panic will keep recurring over and over again. But the good thing is that that too will end.

The end of anxiety and attack is also a critical part of an attack. You should not try to supply it or even make it happen. It will simply end on its own no matter what you believe. Therefore, your role during a panic attack is for you to try and make yourself comfortable as you wait for it to come to an end. However, if you cannot feel comfortable even one bit, then all you have to do is wait for it to end.

But how do I wait for it to end? Here are a few simple techniques that I have used successful along with many other people and am sure they will help you while you wait for your experience to end.

Belly breathing

This is something that you can do irrespective of what happens. Try as much as you can to breathe from your diaphragm up. So many people think that they know how to breathe deeply, but the truth is, they do not do it the right way, and this explains why they fail to get good results. Taking a deep belly breath plays a critical role in helping you calm down and hence ward off the panic attack.

Talk to yourself

You can do this silently from the inside. Try to talk to yourself about the whole situation and what you need to do. Ask yourself whether what is happening is danger or discomfort. Try to practice some of your coping skills. You can tell yourself that the whole situation is just out of fear and you can get through it.

Get involved in the present

The reason why people panic is because they imagine something bad will happen to them in the future or probably something has already happened in the past and they are afraid that it will happen again. This explains why most panic attacks involve the "what if..." questions and thoughts. It is not because your fear is happening now.

The best thing that you can do is to try and get back to what you were doing before the attack happened. This will simply help you get closer to overcoming the attack by simply directing that energy to the present. Simply work with what is in your environment.

Work with your body

During a panic attack, certain parts of the body tend to become tense. Try to identify them and relax. It could be your jaw muscles, back, legs, neck, and shoulders among others. Do not just stand rigid holding your breath because it will make things even worse. If you start feeling that you cannot move, try to start with someplace like your finger or toes and work your way up to the top and until the rest of your body feels relaxed.

Step 4: Repeat

This step is very critical especially when you start experiencing another wave of attack coming. The first reaction often is "Oh my God, it didn't work the first time!" Well, repeating what you have already done before is just to remind you that it is all okay if it that happens. Just try to start from the top and work your way down. The truth is, you may go through quite some cycles before you can experience a positive impact.

Step 5: End

As already mentioned earlier, the end of the panic attack is part of a panic attack. Well, no matter what you do, the truth is that your panic attack will eventually come to an end. This simply means that it is not your role to make it end, but simply make yourself comfortable during the attack as you wait for the end to come to pass. Therefore, the next time you wonder whether it will all end, just tell yourself that it definitely will.

Chapter 4
Grateful & Perspective

Ways of breaking out of anxiety is becoming grateful for what you have and not focusing on what you don't have. I learnt in my 20s that when you are grateful fears disappears and abundance appears, even if you don't have everything you want. I know you can look at areas of your life and feel grateful for the little things but most people get stuck in the paradigm of always wanting more and never feeling grateful.

How often do we get caught up making a living and never feel grateful for everything we have accomplished. If you have bad anxiety right now you should start to feel happier every time you make progress on anything. That's one of the reason I used to feel depressed and anxious and it was because I was like on autopilot and was trying to do better and wasn't realizing the progress that I was making. If I do anything well throughout the day, I will always reflect on it and if I have a bad experience I will reflect and find out the learning in the experience. It's changing your perception and finding the positive in every experience.

When I am feeling depressed and anxious I always know how to break out of it but I want you to know that you will go through this all throughout your life. You will have weeks where you feel incredible and weeks where you need to break out of a slump but if you know the way to break out, you will have more control. I am only giving you ways to think different because this stuff that I'm telling you shifted my life for the better so I want you to have that gift. Some weeks I don't want to do certain things, sometimes I don't want to get up and give 100% but that's when I need to do it the most. If I don't have that willpower and keep building my prefrontal cortex muscle then how am I meant to live my dreams?

Everyone that you see that is so inspiring and confident weren't born like that. They have done rituals like I have told you on a consistent basis and have developed that into their identity. Do they feel anxious and scared at times? Yes absolutely but they don't let it ruin their life because they know by living in that place it will destroy their life. I don't want you to beat yourself up anymore.

Your idea of a problem is someone else's idea of their ultimate dream. Your worse problem has to be put in perspective because if it isn't you'll keep living the same story. There is someone out there that would love to look like you, have your problems and live where you live. There are parts of the world where it would traumatise you to know what they get up to and have to deal with. I think we understand what's going on but we don't emotionally know. I've been over to Africa & parts of America and it's traumatising to see how people live from day to day.

The way I got broke out of depression was I realized you got all eternity to be dead so you may as well just live as happy as you can have & live your life. I started living out of my comfort zone because I live for the rush of feelings. Even if I am feeling negative feelings when I'm out of my comfort zone I believe it makes you feel alive. I got in my head that the only time we feel alive is when we feel emotion and I believe that's why people get addicted to their problems because it makes them feel rushes of emotion.

Most people stay in the same position and hold onto their problems because it gives them significance and comfort. It gives them high negative emotions but understand emotions make you feel. If you take a drug it changes your emotions; it makes you feel good at times and makes you feel depressed at times, it's the same as problems. Our problems can become drugs and that's why it is very scary and weird that someone would hold onto their problems and believe they can't break out of depression. I talked to a lot of people that are masters in helping people with depression and they said the same exact answer as I just said then. There were so many times in my life where I wouldn't want to let go of the problems in my life because they were so attached to my identity.

Haven't you ever wondered why in relationship people get treated badly and they still go back? It's because they are addicted to the emotion they feel. It has nothing to do with the person but to do with the range of emotions, the extreme highs and lows. I want you to realize we can get emotionally addicted to anything and it can be very scary or exciting so always realize this. I had a car salesman's try to sell me a car and I said I just needed to think about it. He rang me consistently and I would give him the same answer 'I'll ring you if I want it, don't push it.' He saw that the positive approach wasn't working so he would try to tear me down saying I'm a bad person and he just needs to chat to me face to face just to sought it all out. It sounds crazy I know but I knew he was trying to make me feel bad so I would get addicted to the emotions. People can easily use this stuff for manipulation and I just want to make you aware of it, so you understand the process.

So perspective is key with this and I want you to start reflecting on everything that you do in a positive way so you get addicted to the emotion of it. Starting out becoming more social to get over social anxiety starts with going out and not particularly doing anything but playing around with your emotions. You have a built in emotional response to going out to a public place you're not familiar with. Everyone has this but the people that look like they got it handled are the ones who have built the skill of managing their emotions.

The antidote that you can start doing for yourself is reflecting on your day before you go to bed at night. Before you go to sleep start reflecting with gratitude about what you learnt and all the little things around you that you feel grateful for. It's training your mind to go there and if you are anxious I know you don't go to this place on a regular basis.

One key that I learned from a mentor was when you feel super stressed about doing something, change your perception of the situation to, 'I feel grateful for this opportunity.' This is the secret and realizing everything in your life is a gift. I really do believe that we are guided with the problems we have and every serious problem that you have is a gift if you really go deep about it. If you can really look back on your life and realize that your worse days are really your best days, your life takes on a whole new meaning. Looking back on my life when I was depressed for years, I say thank god I was depressed for years because if I wasn't I wouldn't be so caring, loving and have the confidence that I have right now. If you can really start doing this with your life I promise you, you'll take life like a game and have fun with it.

Gratitude Exercise

Close your eyes and put your hand on your heart.

Start going back to times in your life that you had happy experiences and feel grateful.

Start feeling grateful for another day of Life

Start going through heaps of great memories in your mind's eye and feel everything.

Chapter 5
Meditation

Meditation has been known to drastically increase a person's ability to control anxious thoughts that trigger panic by teaching you alternative ways to respond to your anxious feelings and worry. Therefore, instead of you dwelling on your negative emotions and fear and letting them control how you respond to situations, you learn how to control your feelings and respond positively to stressful situations.

When we panic, we let the irrational thoughts and emotions that we are feeling control the way we respond to the situation. We make small problems appear bigger and insurmountable, and small decisions become life and death decisions. We focus so much on the problem and our ability to solve it to the point we cannot even remember what caused the problem. The reaction triggers panic, which is what our brain will remember to associate similar situations with, so the next time we are in similar situation, our brain responds by sending our body messages that induce similar panic every time. By meditating, we are learning to take control of our thoughts, to disassociate ourselves briefly with your thoughts so that we can better analyze them later instead of being consumed with the thoughts. Your brain now no longer registers the panicked response; instead, it registers the calm, relaxed response so the next time you are faced with a stressful situation, your brain sends the message to your body to relax and calm down.

Meditation teaches you to calm your mind and slow down your racing thoughts, and to tune in to more positive reinforcement which in turn helps improve your cognitive and learning skills. As you continue to practice meditation, you will start to notice that you are able to focus better and rein in irrational thoughts. If you master meditation, you will be able to notice when your mind wanders off during class or work meetings and be able to rein your thoughts back to the appropriate thing you are supposed to be focusing on.

Meditation can help people suffering from anxiety attacks learn how to let go of control, especially in certain situations where they are surrounded by circumstances beyond their control that trigger their anxiety. For example, as you are preparing to leave your home for the office, you receive a phone call from a friend telling you that your company is going to be laying off staff. The phone call disrupts your routine and you leave the house five minutes later than you planned, and as you reach the bus stop you find that the bus was early today and that the next bus is going to be coming in the next thirty minutes, which means you will be late to work.

Your natural response is to panic. You have just heard that your company is lying off people, you wonder if you are now one of them and you will not have a job, which will make you unable to pay rent, which will make your landlord evict you, and then you will have to live in the streets. Your thoughts have made you blow the situation out of proportion, which induces more panic that makes you unable to handle the situation. If you are someone who regularly practices meditation, you will realize after you miss the bus that you have other options. You can call someone and see if they will be able to drop you, or you can call your boss and explain that you are running a few minutes late. You realize that you can remain calm even if you are stuck in a bad situation.

To start meditating, look for a quiet place where you will not be disturbed or easily distracted. Focus all your thoughts on one object or word; you can also choose just a sound such as "mmh" and gently repeat that word or sound for around twenty minutes. Some people find it beneficial to use their breathing pattern as something they can focus on for the stipulated twenty minutes. Basically, in meditation, what you are doing is quieting your mind and allowing it to focus on one thing at a time. This process of meditation can help you learn how to process your thoughts when you panic. For instance, when you are called to give a presentation at school or at the office and your thoughts tell you that people will laugh at what you will say, or that you are not adequately prepared, then you reinforce those thoughts by seeing yourself fainting or forgetting everything. Notice that by this time your thoughts and feeling are out of sync with the reality — nobody has heard your presentation so how can they think it's stupid? To gain control of our emotions, we need to learn to distract ourselves from negative thoughts.

Chapter 6
Increasing Your Self-Awareness

You may have noticed that there is a theme that is going on when it comes to increasing your own emotional intelligence. This theme is all about helping you to recognize what is going on in your own life, such as your emotional triggers, so you can be ready when they come up in day-to-day life.

Introspection is a skill that those with high emotional intelligence will naturally possess. Not everyone will be born with this skill, but it is something that you can work on over time. One of the first questions that you should ask yourself is "How do I know that I need to be more self-aware?" To figure this out, take a look at the way that you have behaved recently. Have you made mistakes, let your emotions taken over, or done and said things that you later regret? If you have, then that means it is time to work on your self-awareness.

It is important not to focus on the negatives during this exercise. Everyone makes mistakes or does things they regret but recognizing that you have done these and that you need to work on them is the first step forward.

Focus on where you want to go, not where you have been. Let's take a look at some of the steps you can take to raise your own self-awareness.

Developing self-awareness

To start, you need to take some time to be by yourself. Maybe set aside half an hour or so for this and bring along a pen and paper; sometimes it helps if you are able to write down all of your thoughts and feelings. When you are ready, it is time to take a look at some of your patterns of action and thought. Some of the things that you can consider asking yourself during this period include:

• Why do you enjoy the entertainment that you choose?

• What features attracted you to the people that you love?

• What makes you avoid doing certain things?

• What are some of your values and what do you want out of life? What do you not want?

• What are your thoughts on lying? Are your morals and character clear?

- Are you a generally happy person or do you act tired and stressed all of the time? How might these emotions be interpreted by others?

- How do you think others perceive you?

Once you have had some time to answer the questions in the last section, it is time to move on to do an examination of your attitudes. Often your attitudes about a situation are going to be based on your expectations, which are often exaggerated by your emotions or are otherwise unrealistic. Having an attitude that is positive is going to help you out so much more compared to a negative attitude because it will help you to gain strength to deal with any situation you encounter.

An example of holding onto negative attitudes occurs when it comes to your own potential. Just saying the words "I can't do that" will limit your potential and once you say the words, you never will accomplish your goals. You would be surprised at what you are capable of doing if you just put your mind to it. If you switch your thinking around to "I can do that!" you will see that you can push yourself so much further than you originally believed.

Some people who are working on their own self-awareness will choose to keep some form of a journal. They will keep track of their feelings, their day, or any other information that they deem important. After some time, take a look through the journal again and you may find out that some attitudes or events that you have will lead to others. You can also see that many of the things that you overreacted to in the past are not that important now, and it may lead you to reexamine some of the ways you react to similar events in the future.

And finally, you need to make sure to learn how to acknowledge your actions. This one can be hard, especially if you are not all that proud of the actions that you were taking. But you have to acknowledge your actions, even when they are not bringing you the results that you want. When you start to notice that an action isn't making you feel good or it is not getting you to a place you want to be, you may start to react in a different way.

Self-awareness through the perceptions of others

The second part of this process is to learn how to find your own self-awareness based on the way that others perceive you. If possible, take some time to ask your family and friends how they perceive you. In most cases, you will probably need to spend time asking yourself questions though, since most of the time those closest to you will have a hard time answering these questions. Some of the questions that you should be asking yourself concerning your character and identity include:

- Do I spend time smiling or mostly frowning?
- Is my handshake firm when I meet someone new?
- Do I have trouble making eye contact with people?
- What are some characteristics of my walk?
- Do I stand up tall or do I slouch?

Once you have been able to talk to a few people about their perception of you (but make sure you are working with people who are going to give you honest opinions), and you have your own answers, it is time to analyze the feedback. With this feedback, you will be able to go about the process of addressing the answers you don't like. For example, you can work on standing up taller or looking people in the eyes when they talk to you. You can work on smiling instead of frowning. Each person will have different points to work on and you will be able to personalize your plan to meet what perceptions you want to change.

Staying aware

Finally, it is important that once you have received your feedback and made some of the small changes, you learn how to stay aware of how you are thinking and acting. This is going to help you in so many ways including being aware of your perceptions and the emotions that otherwise would take over your life.

The first thing that you should work on is to gauge your progress during the day. You can take just five minutes at some point during the day to see if you are reaching your goals. Did you try smiling more or do you need to do a bit better? Did you stand up tall when you walked? You may have a few different characteristics that you want to work on, but just focus on one at a time. Often one will tie into the others and you will automatically start doing them all in response.

And finally, you need to develop your own attitude of mindfulness so that you are aware that there are things that go on beyond your private little world. Many of the problems that arise with our emotions occur because we have learned how to be on autopilot and we just react when things don't go the way that we would like. When we learn that not everything is important, that some people react because they had a bad day and not because of anything to do with us, we can gain a better control of our own emotions.

Chapter 7
Meditation And Mindfulness

One of the best things that you can do when it comes to improving your emotional intelligence is focusing on yourself. Often the reason that your emotions are not behaving the way that you would like is that you have some sort of inner turmoil, whether it is stress or something else, that makes it really hard for you to relax and let the little things go. One way that you can help focus the mind is through meditation and mindfulness. Let's take some time to look at these two techniques and how they could help you feel better.

Meditation

To get started with this one, you will need to set aside about fifteen minutes each day, or twice a day if you feel you would benefit from it, where you won't be interrupted at all. Pick out a nice quiet room and get yourself comfortable. A pillow to sit on, a blanket in case you get cold, and a timer to help keep track of time if you need to be somewhere (so you don't focus on the clock), can all be tools to help you out.

When you are ready, sit down on the floor with your legs crossed and your back nice and straight. This gives you a good alignment that will help the airflow through your body as you breathe. If sitting on the floor is uncomfortable or you can't do it, it is just fine to sit on a chair, as long as you keep your feet flat on the floor and sit up straight. Your hands can just rest in your lap.

Now close your eyes and start some steady breathing in and out. Your breathing may be a little fast at first, but try to concentrate all of your energy on getting it to slow down a bit. The deep breaths should help to fill your body with good energy while the exhales will dispel all that bad energy.

The goal during this is to try and just think about your deep breathing. For beginners, this is going to be hard. You are used to keeping your mind going all of the time, and giving up on that and clearing out the brain completely is going to seem impossible. The good news is that this will happen, it just takes some time. If your mind begins to wander, and it is sure to do this in the beginning, just gently bring it back to focusing on your breath. Don't feel bad that it went off course or get mad at yourself for this mental transgression. Having these emotions will just make it harder to get the benefits.

For some people, just concentrating on their breathing is not going to be enough. This is where some other forms of meditation can come into play. Some people will repeat or think about a word that they can concentrate on, some will bring in some gentle music, or you can purchase a guided meditation to help focus. All of these can be great choices because they still help you to relax and get your mind off the things that are bothering it in real life.

You will find that meditation is able to help out in many different aspects of your life. Not only will it help you to become more connected with your emotions and become self-aware of what is going on with you, but some people use it to help promote better sleep, to help them relax, and it is a great tool to help with anxiety and stress. No matter what method you use meditation for, you are going to see a ton of great benefits in the process.

Mindfulness

The idea with mindfulness is that you start to take things a bit slower. Rather than rushing through life like most of us do, you will take a moment to really savor what is going on. You could pretend that you have been in a coma for twenty years and are finally coming out of it. How would you experience the world again?

While many of us are so busy with our daily lives that we barely have time to notice the things around us, mindfulness asks us to stop for a bit and start to see what is there. You can spend five minutes doing this a day or try to add it in as much as possible, but it won't take long before you see the benefits.

When mindfulness is added into your life, even for a short period of time, you will quickly start to see noticeable results. You will start to appreciate the little things that happen and let go of some of the big things because they no longer matter. Many times, you will start to appreciate what you have and just enjoy life in a way that you never thought possible before.

If you would like to start with mindfulness, pick one activity each day that you want to do mindfully. Let's say that you want to practice mindfulness when you are brushing your teeth. If so, then each day when you brush your teeth, you will start to pay more attention to the activity, rather than rushing through it without giving it much thought. You will notice the feel of your toothbrush in your hand, the taste of the toothpaste, the foam that forms, how the bristles feel on your teeth and even how clean the teeth feel when you are done. You only need to spend a few minutes on this each day, but it will make a big difference.

Let's take a moment to try out an exercise to see how mindfulness can work and to help you to get started. Pick one meal during the day where you don't have to rush to finish. Sit down at the table and keep distractions to a minimum. For this one, it is also best if you are able to eat alone.

During this meal, you are going to try and take in as many different sensations as you can. First, you are going to concentrate on the food that you are eating. With each bite, we will notice the texture of the food, the taste, and how your body reacts to it. Chew at least ten times with each bite so that you can enjoy savoring the food rather than just rushing through it.

You don't want to just concentrate on the food though, take into account the other sensations that are around you. Think about the smells, whether they come from the food, candles that you light, or somewhere else in the room. If you turned on some music, enjoy the notes that are coming in your direction while you enjoy the food. Take a look at the table that is around you and just enjoy the sights.

This is meant to turn your dining time into an experience. We often rush through a meal, trying to get it done as soon as possible so we can hurry on to the next thing. But for this activity, take as much time as you can to savor the full experience. Really enjoy what is going on around you. It may seem a bit laborious at first, but the point is to help you recognize what is going on around you in the simple activities of your life.

By the time you are done with the meal, you will have enjoyed it in a manner that you may not have imagined in the past. Try to do this at least once or twice a week, if you don't have time to do it every night.

It is going to make such a big difference in your outlook on life and can help you to gain more control over your emotions as well.

Meditation and mindfulness can both make a big difference in your life. They will help you to take a step back from the day to day and focus on all of the good things, the important things that are there, rather than all the little things that often take up all of your attention. When you are able to add both of these into your life even if you can only do them for a few minutes each day, you are sure to see some amazing results in no time.

Chapter 8
How To Get Rid Of Unpleasant Memories With EMDR

The EMDR method is especially effective for processing unpleasant memories and negative experiences of the past. The protocol for the use of EMDR in this case is as follows.

Step 1. Choose a goal to work out - an unpleasant episode or a memory from the past.

Example: when I was 4 years old, I sledded and ran into another child. I rolled over, and I was covered with his sled. I cut my hand about them, and I was bleeding.

Step 2. Think about what kind of visual image appears in your head when you think about it.

First comes up the moment before the collision, when I rush right at that guy. And then I remember the blood on my hand, it was terribly unpleasant.

For study method, I suggest choosing one specific picture, usually the one that causes the most unpleasant feelings. In this case, this is a picture of blood.

Step 3. Pay attention to what feelings you have when you visualize this picture, and what is the intensity of these feelings on a 10-point scale, where 0 - I feel nothing, and 10 - I feel the greatest possible discomfort.

"Looking" at my bloodied hand, I experience fear and a very sharp, unpleasant feeling, which I cannot describe in words. As if everything is bad inside ... On a 9 on a 10-point scale.

Here the preparatory stage is completed, now we go directly to the work.

Step 4. Actually desensitization using eye movements

Imagine the picture you have chosen for study, immerse yourself in the sensations that it causes you. And then begin to quickly move your eyes left and right, as described earlier in the section "Description of the EMDR method". Perform about 20 such movements and return to the picture again. Pay attention to all the details of the visual image. Have there been any changes? Pay attention to your condition. Has the nature or intensity of the sensations changed? Re-evaluate the intensity of sensations on a 10-point scale.

In our example, after the first round of eye movements, the picture seemed to move slightly. The intensity of the unpleasant feeling almost did not change; it was at 9 - maybe, at 8 and a half.

After the second round, the picture got even further and seemed to blur. There was no more fear; the unpleasant sensation became a little different - more bodily, as if the stomach was being compressed into a lump.

After the third round, the picture is completely flat and almost unrealistic, it has moved a little down, has become smaller in size. Unpleasant feeling is 5 out of 10.

Desensitization is repeated as many times as necessary until the intensity of the discomfort becomes zero. People usually say the following: "Now, when I think about this moment, it does not bother me at all. I still remember the situation well, but the feeling is that it just was and that's it, it doesn't bother me anymore."

After you have worked on one picture, you can take another one. In our example, one traumatic event corresponded to two different emotionally tense pictures - the moment before the collision and blood on the arm. As a result of the elaboration of both pictures, the memory was transformed and ceased to bother the person.

Step 5. Pay attention to bodily sensations. Mentally scan your body for residual tension, muscle blocks, and tightness. If you find a residual discomfort in the body, you can use it as a target for further work.

Step 6. Ask yourself: what conclusion did I make about myself, about others, or about the world as a result of this unpleasant event? In such cases, we often draw conclusions, which we then extend to all similar situations. These findings, backed up by negative experience, become our beliefs. And we are guided by them in later life, often without even realizing ourselves in this report and without subjecting them to critical analysis.

There are a great many examples of such beliefs.

For example, you were bitten by a dog, and now you are afraid of dogs. Although you understand that dogs are not as dangerous as it seems to you, you still cannot get rid of this fear. Your conclusion: dogs are dangerous.

Beliefs are worked out in the same way as all other negative emotions and feelings. First, you should focus on thoughts, and then make a series of eye movements. After that, you should evaluate how strong this thought is on a 10-point scale. Usually, a belief loses its strength and transforms in 2-3 rounds of development with the help of EMDR.

In step 6, work through all the negative thoughts that you have from an incident - one after the other, until they are completely gone.

Step 7. Think about the future. Do you have a concern that well-developed fear may return? If so, use the image of the future as a target for further work.

Step 8. Create a positive image of the future. Imagine a new self, free from anxiety and fears, imagine what your life will be like - and again move your eyes. Do not be afraid, a positive image will not be destroyed as a result of the action of EMDR, most likely, it will become more clear and realistic. This is a very important step, because it allows you to identify possible resistance to positive changes, if present.

Try to create the most vivid and realistic positive image of the future. This will accelerate the positive changes in your life.

Depending on the situation, all seven steps can take you from 15 minutes to an hour and a half, and sometimes even up to several days, work. Do not overload your eyes, if you use EMDR every day. The practice time should not exceed 20 minutes; otherwise it can become too much stress. Do not forget that you can use the technique of emotional freedom without time limits. If you feel that your eyes are tired, and the development of negative emotions is in full swing, use EFT to complete the process and stabilize your emotional state.

Chapter 9
Common Difficulties In Using The EMDR Method

Q.: I do not have time to simultaneously present an unpleasant picture and move my eyes.

A.: You do not have to think about the picture while you are making eye movements. You focus on it at the beginning, and then you can completely concentrate on the movements themselves and upon their completion return to the picture again.

Q.: I chose one picture for study, but after the first round of movements, another one appeared in front of my eyes, also unpleasant, but connected with a completely different situation. Should I continue to work on the original picture or take on a new one?

A.: In such cases, it's recommended trusting your internal process. If a new picture has arisen spontaneously, it is worth working with it. Exercise it until it ceases to cause any discomfort. After that, return to the originally selected goal with which you started work.

Q.: I do not remember the situation completely. I have only a vague or fragmentary memory.

A.: Absolute accuracy is not required at all. Take in the work that material is available to you at the moment. Even fragmentary memories can be effectively worked out with the help of EMDR. In some situations, after 2-3 rounds of EMDR, the picture takes on more specific outlines, and additional details that you did not remember before may begin to appear in it. But this is not necessary. When you can't remember the situation completely, pay more attention to the feelings that it causes you.

Q.: After 2 rounds of EMDR, the picture remained unchanged, and the intensity of unpleasant sensations only increased.

A.: This is really possible: the process of working through negative information occurs through a temporary intensification of an unpleasant feeling. This is natural and happens when a person tries to keep an unpleasant feeling at a distance from himself. We have already discussed issues of resistance to feelings and the importance of their acceptance before, when we talked about the technique of emotional freedom. When working with the EMDR method, (similar to working with EFT) it is important not to resist the unpleasant sensations associated with the images that you are working on.

Q.: The intensity of the sensations is too high. When I try to work out the situation, I have such strong feelings that I just can't continue. I am afraid that in this case I will become even worse.

A.: In such a situation, use the technique of emotional freedom (EFT) in order to relieve the senses and stabilize your condition. Perhaps you still have too few resources to work out precisely this traumatic moment. In this case, temporarily postpone work with this episode. While working out less difficult memories for you, use EFT to learn how to better regulate your current state - all this will allow you to increase your stress resistance resource. After a while, you will be able to return to working out the hardest memories. An alternative is to seek professional help from a specialist who has experience working with severe emotional injuries.

Chapter 10
"8 Simple Exercises"

Do physical activity

The definition of physical activity in this context has not been limited only to exercise. Physical activity is any activity that engages your physique. Mostly it will lead to perspiration. When an individual engages in physical activity, he or she is obliged to concentrate fully on that particular activity. Exercising is a very renowned way to counter depression. Regular exercise has time and again been used as an anti-depressant. When one is exercising, endorphins are boosted. These are chemicals that enable an individual to feel good.

The statistics of how many people deal with stress is always on the upward. When one experiences stress, it has a lasting effect in their lives since it cuts across what an individual is engaging in at a particular time. To eradicate stress completely is an uphill task, and one would rather manage it. Exercising is one of the best methods to manage stress. Many medical practitioners advise that individuals should engage in exercises in a bid to manage stress levels.

The advantages that come with a person engaging in exercises have far been established to be a counter-measure against diseases and as a method of enhancing the body's physical state. Research has it that exercising helps a great deal when decreasing fatigue and enhancing the body's consciousness to the environment. Stress invades the whole of your body, affecting both the body and mind. When this happens, the act of your mind feeling well will be pegged on the act of the body feeling well too. When one is in the act of exercising, the brain produces endorphins which act naturally as pain relievers. They also improve the instances upon which an individual falls asleep. When the body is able to rest, this means that its amounts of anxiety have dropped by a large margin. Production of endorphins can also be triggered by the following practices. They include but are not limited to meditation and breathing deeply. Participation in exercise regularly has proven an overall tension reliever.

Doing relaxation exercises

Another method of reducing stress levels is through the use of some relaxation techniques.

A relaxation technique is any procedure that is of aid to an individual when trying to calm down the levels of anxiety. Stress is effectively conquered when the body itself is responding naturally to the stress levels in the body. Relaxation can be often confused with laying on a couch after a hard day. This relaxation is best done in the form of self-meditation, although its effects are not fulfilling on the impact of stress. Most relaxation techniques are done at the convenience of your home with only an app.

Settling on the right technique for relieving stress is not easy. It is key that you focus on one that is not only favorable to your lifestyle but also your budget. There are various techniques for mind relaxation, which are:

Deep breathing

When breathing deeply, one increases the neuron-transmitters known as endorphins that seek to bring about a feeling of easiness. This technique forms the basis for other types of techniques. In order to achieve this, one needs to sit in a posture that allows his or her back to be straight. One hand should be firmly placed on the chest and the other on the stomach.

An individual should inhale through the nostrils and exhale through the mouth. This procedure should be carried out cyclically and repetitive.

Continuous muscle relaxation

This happens in a two-phase kind of arrangement in that there are the contraction and relaxation of muscles. One phase entails tensing the muscles while the other involves relaxing them. This type of stress reliever works best when you ascend all the way up from your legs. Normally you should have lost clothing on with no shoes. You should take your time to practice the shifts in breathing. Commence with your right foot then your left making sure that you feel every moment of it. The movement should be in ascension, making sure you touch every muscle in your body.

Vision of peace

Our eyes need to be shut during this particular exercise. Here, you close your eyes and see yourself in a state that is devoid of any technicalities. You need to see yourself in a place where you are enjoying yourself to the fullest. Experience peace at its peak. Enjoy the surrounding, for instance, the clean air, the warm sun rays, the friendly water. Feel as your anxiety drifts away, leaving you at peace. After that, you can then open your eyes gently and come back to real facts.

Calculated movements

Like meditation, exercising the mind through calculated movements entails engaging the mind on the events of the present. Whereas meditation focuses on the past, exercising the mind is akin to the current situations. Take, for instance, yoga or the famous Tai chi. These movements are done in a synchronized manner, one that enables the mind to relax. When the mind is relaxing, levels of stress fall.

Write

Writing is one of the many solutions to stress relief. Writing helps reduce stress levels to individuals with anxiety disorders since jotting down your horrible experiences is one way of parting with them completely. The type of writing that focuses on the previous events that might have taken place in the life of a person is referred to as writing in the form of expression. This is because the writer is trying to connect with the readers through opening up to them, telling them what he or she has been through. This type of writing may not be effective for every individual.

Some individuals may be inclined to be haunted over and over again by what they are writing. This may cause more harm than good. With writing, one tends to evaluate the situation in different ways despite the outcome.

Apart from writing as a form of expression, there is another form of writing which entails that you write from a reflective point of view. With this type of view, an individual is able to visualize the situation differently. With this kind of writing, the writer is able to unearth various things that he or she had not put into consideration. With writing, it can be so confidential that an individual is able to write what he or she is ashamed of saying out to other people. People who write about particular events in their lives are the ones that spearhead the solution process.

Managing time in the right way for you

Here stress levels are brought about by timelines that we seek to meet in order to fulfill our obligations. All around the world, we are defined by the various responsibilities that are tied to us by the inherent nature of existence.

Some of us are parents, and at the same time, have demanding jobs in a bid to make ends meet. Juggling between being a parent and being apt at your place of work is not an easy task. It will always leave you worn out if not stressed.

The old saying that time is money has never been side-shadowed at any ounce. The kind of life that an individual is leading will always be defined by the kind of life that a particular individual is leading. How best an individual manages time determines the degree of how best an individual leads his or her life. For instance, it is common sense that the body needs to rest in order to rejuvenate. To do this, the body requires at least eight hours to seven hours of sleep.

Spend time with animals

Research has it that interacting with pets, or friendly animals have a calming effect on the levels of stress that an individual has. Research has it that most mental illnesses have been curbed by pets. Co-habiting with a pet comes with a bag of goodies that include uncompromised companionship. A pet will always be there by your side even when you are feeling lonely; the feeling will be eradicated.

Pets have time and again been used as a means of getting to know each other and making friends. With a pet in place, you are inclined to form social networks that will help you connect with other people regularly. With pets around, one's blood pressure is reduced to manageable levels; your overall cardiovascular health is improved. With a pet running here and there, we will always be obliged to exercise often when playing with them. When interacting with a pet, you feel like you are having a conversation with a normal human being. This, in turn, has two effects. First is that we will not experience loneliness. We will also be inclined to forget about the worse thoughts rather than dwelling on them.

Stay in the open air

The breathing of fresh air has a lot of positive effects on our bodies. Our bodies depend on the process of breathing in order to live progressively. Having a feel of clean air or a sensation of petals aids in the alleviation of stress. The levels of serotonin produced in the body are affected by the amounts of oxygen in the body. A higher level of serotonin leads to a hyped feeling of being amazed. For instance, the sensation found in lavender aids in the reduction of insomnia. Jasmine plant, on the other hand, has been used as a boost to mood.

Research has it that failure of exposure to clean air can be a cause of death. This was after a report was released with individuals succumbing to death due to polluted air. Fresh air enhances strength in the body. The respiration process that occurs in the production of energy has it that oxygen is a raw material. Fatigue comes as a result of not being exposed to fresh air for long periods of time.

Digestion is also a key aspect when it comes to fresh air. Taking a stroll allows the body to engage in a series of reactions that will enhance the digestion to take place faster. This is opposed to the habit of eating at your office desk as you continue with your task. The digestion here is curtailed, and thus, it affects the concentration levels of a particular individual. This person is obliged not to function for a longer period without getting fatigued.

The open-air exposes our lungs to fresh air. Smoking darkens our lungs and puts us at danger of cancer. The sensation of clean air in our lungs is relieving in the sense that you are feeling every part of your air sacks. This also aids in the eradication of sputum from our chests that will, in turn, lead to blockages.

Research has it that exposure to clean air provides the requisite bacteria that is responsible for fighting off germs that cause diseases. Germs are often the causative agents of various diseases. Fresh air in eradicating this germs, maintains the status core of the body keeping you healthy. The combination of freshwater with clean air incomparable. With this in place, your stress levels will drop subsequently.

Chapter 11
Improving Ineffective Communication Skills

Networking and communication skills are vital skills you must learn to succeed in life today. Opportunities are continuously available at the workplace, at home, in church, you name it. Whenever you engage in a social construct, you find yourself in need of the right communication skills. These determine how well you get along with the people in your environment.

At each stage in life, you encounter different groups of people. Some people come into your life and walk away, only for fate to make your paths cross again at some point. Lack of proper communication skills can make it difficult for you to reconnect with people you were once close to, especially after spending so many years away from them. This explains why you would find every reason not to attend a reunion party.

Professionally, networking has become an essential part of our careers. You are invited to events all the time, and you interact with lots of people. You must maintain a good image for your company and your brand. Always remember that your individual presence represents the image of your company, and you must learn how to espouse the goals, objectives, vision, and mission of your company in these engagements.

While this might be overwhelming, it is possible through CBT. One of the most important skills in communication is to understand the behavior of other people around you and healthily respond to them. Effective communication relies on proper listening and the appropriate consequential response to the message you receive.

If you do not listen properly, you will often fail to get important information. Other than that, problems will catch you unawares when they arise. Listening is an effective way of understanding people, understanding their view of the world through their words, and helps improve communication between you and them. Listening also enables you to nurture and foster healthy relationships, whether you are making new ones or rekindling old ones.

Psychology of Listening

People love to be appreciated. This is why they respond better to those who listen to them. Listening and understanding what someone is talking about is a sign of emotional intelligence. Fostering quality relationships with people around you will depend on how well you can listen and communicate with them. You can learn these skills.

You must also know that to listen, you have to be keen and focus on what someone is telling you. Try to avoid pseudo-listening, which happens when you can hear someone but you can barely understand what they are talking about. Chances are high that you have other ideas in mind keeping you distracted, such as:

Passing time until your opportunity to speak comes up

Seeking vulnerabilities in the other person's speech

Pretending to listen so you are likable

Pre-emptive listening, where you are only alert for specific information, but blocking out everything else that you hear

Trying to find out whether you are getting the response you desire from your audience

Looking for weak points in an argument that you can use to intimidate the audience

You might have experienced these distractions from time to time. You might think you are smart and sharp, but in the long run, someone who has effective communication skills will figure you out. Some people might call you out on your flaws.

Improving Your Communication Skills

To develop your communication skills, you need to examine yourself and identify the factors that are hindering your communication with those around you. You get used to most of these factors and barely notice them. These factors are the listening blocks.

People use listening blocks all the time and they make it difficult to communicate effectively with their audience. Once you identify these blocks, you can take steps to change them and improve. Making even subtle changes will eventually help you learn to listen and engage your audience better.

Stop Reading Minds

Instead of listening to someone, you are busy trying to figure out what they feel or what they are thinking. The problem with mind reading is that you never listen to the conversation around you. Instead, you are only waiting for cues and clues. This form of mental filtration makes you assume the reactions and intentions of people you are engaging.

Drawing Comparisons

Another trait you need to change is making comparisons between the speaker and yourself. Comparisons divert your attention from the subject matter, and instead, you focus on mundane things like how attractive the person is, whether they are funny or not, whether you are better at what they are saying or doing than they are. Since you are too busy trying to measure up, you miss the important discussion going on.

Pre-Judging

Many people are guilty of this one. Instead of starting a conversation on a clean slate, you have already formed an opinion of the speaker, of their message and intentions. Pre-judgment happens especially for individuals you have interacted with earlier or read about. You will barely focus on the conversation they are having with you because you have already decided they are too stubborn to meet your needs, writing them off in the process. Unfortunately, even if every opinion you have about them is valid, this might be that rare occasion where they do something out of the ordinary and you miss it.

Strong Debates

How often do you listen to someone instead of arguing with them? Many people barely listen to you when you speak to them. Instead, they take the first few words you say and turn it into an argument. In so doing, the focus of the conversation will be looking for points you can use in an argument or points that can win you the discussion instead of getting the message in the conversation.

Having such arguments in a conversation stems from having strong opinions about yourself or your ideas, preferences, and beliefs. Therefore, anyone who mentions anything which is not in line with what you consider the norm will not have a relaxed conversation with you. You should learn to listen and let someone finish what they are saying.

This gives you time to evaluate their content and then make up your mind before raising an argument.

Giving Advice

You might be the type of person who barely lets someone complete a sentence before interjecting with some words of advice or dropping suggestions. You always feel you have so much more to offer, and the more you keep this up, people will feel you do not consider their opinions.

The problem with this is that, over time, you only get to hear the words that someone speaks to you but miss the emotions in the conversation. Someone might be trying to open up to you about something they are passionate about, or a personal problem, but you dismiss them even before they get to the point of comfort.

This is a concern that is shared a lot between superiors and their juniors, and over time, people find it difficult to talk to you about their problems. However much you try to get them to open up and talk to you about their struggles, they already know you will dismiss them.

Low Confidence

Low confidence is one of the underlying reasons behind depression and anxiety. Since you do not have faith in your ability, you cannot take risks. You handle tasks assigned to you half-heartedly because you cannot find the energy or courage to give anything your best shot. You have convinced yourself for a long time that you do not have the guts to do anything correctly.

These thought patterns eventually end up affecting your performance. Over time, your brain enforces this lack of confidence in your ability, and it becomes a vicious cycle you can barely get out of.

In CBT, your therapist uses a combination of methods to change your dysfunctional thought process. They try to do away with the negative thought patterns that have kept you stuck and hold you back from realizing your potential.

Negative, ineffective behavior and self-defeatist thoughts are just some things that end up causing low confidence. Your therapist will try to teach you how to behave and think like someone who has a strong belief in their ability, someone confident about their contribution to their environment.

CBT Interventions for Low Confidence

Cognitive Restructuring

Cognitive restructuring is an intervention where your therapist identifies your negative thought process. They focus on the negative assumptions you have made about yourself and help you find a better way of tackling difficult situations.

For someone low on confidence, cognitive restructuring is mainly about dealing with the assumptions you have made about your inability to perform, your failure to accomplish tasks, and the harsh judgments you keep passing on yourself. It is about helping you find a positive, useful, and realistic way of thinking about situations you engage in each day.

Systematic Exposure

Systematic exposure is about facing your demons. If you have low confidence, it is easy to run away from certain situations you are worried about. The concept of systematic exposure builds on the pretext that by avoiding situations that fill you with fear, you are holding yourself back from evaluating your abilities.

If you do not try, you might never know how you would have performed. Perhaps you are not as bad as you think you are. Perhaps you are the best person for the job. But since you are afraid to try and you keep running away from it, you will never know for sure.

Through systematic exposure, your therapist encourages you to open up and face the situations you continuously avoid. By dealing with these situations, you will realize that you are not as bad as you had otherwise imagined.

You realize that things are not as difficult as you thought they were, and this makes you more confident. It helps you overcome anxiety in such situations. For low confidence, systematic exposure involves working with your therapist to plan activities you would typically avoid. After planning, you must frequently power through these activities.

Your therapist might ask you to try speaking up in meetings or debating. The more you practice these activities, the easier it will be for you to muster the courage to be bolder in your interactions.

Mindfulness Training

Mindfulness is a skill that helps you focus on your present. Often, you find your mind wandering, thinking about things you cannot influence, worrying, or deep in thought. The problem with this is that you fight yourself often. You give yourself a difficult time as you keep second-guessing yourself.

Through mindfulness training, you will learn to give yourself a breather. In a difficult situation, you focus on how to improve your confidence. Even if you fail at what you are doing, you should not let it get you down. Dust yourself off and move on.

Mindfulness training also goes hand in hand with solution-finding. If you are low on confidence, you will continuously see yourself as a victim. There are many situations you find yourself in which you can get out of. However, since you are not confident in your ability to find solutions to your problems, you wallow in pain and grief. An unhealthy status quo should not manifest longer than necessary. Believe in yourself and in your ability to find a solution.

CBT Exercises for Low Confidence

Feeling good about yourself and your ability demands internal effort. Your therapist will help you find realistic ways to deal with the things you worry about, the ones that are holding you back. Together, you will identify the patterns that exist in your brain about your confidence and try to change them and use the new patterns you learn to improve your confidence.

Exercise 1: Perspective

At times, you feel you are only as good as other people say you are. This is not true. The truth is that you should define your strength based on your criteria and not a vague reality that has been forced onto you by someone else. You know your strengths and weaknesses.

There is nothing wrong with reflecting or comparing yourself with someone as long as you do not take it too far. Comparisons should help you challenge yourself to do better and improve yourself, not cause you to doubt your abilities.

There are situations in your environment that might make it difficult to thrive, hurting your confidence.

These are the moments you should discuss with your therapist and find a way of conquering them.

Note down a few aspects of your day that are challenging. Write down the positive things you have done that day, things you conquered, and how it made you feel. Look at the list, and the sentiments attached and list them in order of those that made you feel most important and appreciated.

You will notice that the things which concern your personality rank highest. This might seem obvious but it means that confidence is all about perspective and perceptions. This acts as a reminder that the core of your self-confidence depends more on the effort you make personally than on what others think about you. The accomplishments you made, especially with challenging tasks, are all dependent on your ability. It is your self-belief that keeps getting you through.

Exercise 2: Criticism

You are your own worst enemy. Few people find as many faults with you as you do. You criticize yourself often. Even when you work hard, you still feel you did not do your best. You can change the way you talk to yourself. Instead of the negative thoughts, you can change the narrative and replace it with positive and realistic dialogue.

Encourage yourself to go the extra mile. Appreciate the effort you are making and believe that tomorrow will be a better day. You might not always have a good day, but giving up should never be an option.

Stand in front of a mirror and talk to yourself. Listen to the words that come to mind. How critical are you? Reflect upon those words. Do they remind you of someone in particular? Do they remind you of something you have heard for a long time?

While reflecting on those words, ask yourself how valid they are. Do you believe they are an accurate representation of your current predicament? Rethink those narratives and imagine you were saying them to your friend, younger siblings, or even your child. What tone would you use? Now look into the mirror again and use the exact tone you would use, but this time, speak to yourself. You would probably try to use a reassuring voice when advising someone. Why then, do you criticize yourself? Treat yourself with the same care you would offer someone else.

When you practice internal dialogue and make it consistent and supportive, it is easy to change the way you see yourself. Instead of trying to fix yourself because of your constant criticism, you can make peace with the person you are. Work with what you have.

When you wake up in the morning, assure yourself you will be the best version of yourself that day. In your internal dialogue, be kind to yourself. Life is already hard enough—why make things harder?

Exercise 3: Perfection

It is easy to confuse organization with perfection. You come across people who seem to get things right all the time. Through your interactions with these individuals, you feel they are perfect. Perfection is a fallacy that consumes most people and you should not worry about it.

You focus a lot on the good things that someone else does, the success they achieve, without looking at their journey to get there. We are a result-oriented generation. Everyone seems to be excited about the destination but ignore the journey.

No one is perfect. The sooner you get that into your head, the sooner you will start appreciating yourself for who you are. This will also help you improve your confidence. You need to believe in your ability, especially if you did your best. You must also acknowledge that you might be unable to show up with the same level of enthusiasm and energy tomorrow as you did yesterday.

People have bad days they barely talk about. Those in their immediate circles may or may not know about that. The same applies to you. Do not focus so much on the result that you lose track of the process.

Processes can be daunting. Some processes drain all the energy out of you; some even drain the life out of you. However, believe in yourself. This is the only thing that matters. Alter your perception of perfection for reality. You must be honest about your abilities, the things you can do and how you can do them. Once you are honest with yourself, it is easier to appreciate your input and be more confident.

Chapter 12
Find Your Core Issues

This is because we are covering the core of your problems, which is the most important and essential step to healing your anxiety and depression and other life issues. Finding the core of your pain is hard, and addressing this core is even tougher. But you cannot heal yourself if you do not first address the true cause of your issues. You can treat and mask symptoms all that you want, yet they will still manifest when you don't expect it until you get rid of their root cause.

For some people, the cause of their depression or anxiety is obvious. It is related to a health problem, hormonal imbalance, or even a brain injury that disrupted the chemical balance in the brain. It is easy to find these problems through blood tests and other relevant medical tests.

Other people know the source of their problems. They know that a trauma or loss that they suffered, abuse that they endured, or some other painful past event that once happened to them lies at the very bottom of their suffering. However, they do not want to address this problem because it hurts too much. This avoidance is understandable but it is very counterproductive. Not addressing these issues will result in the problem never being corrected.

Some people are not lucky enough to know what their core issues are. They struggle with depression and anxiety and can't find helpful treatments. If you are one of these people, you probably keep trying to treat your anxiety and depression, with no luck. There appears to be nothing wrong with you physically, and you can't think of any traumatic events in your past that would explain your constant suffering. There is probably a deep, internal source lying at the bottom of your anxiety or depression. You may believe schemas about yourself that keep your self-esteem low. You may feel like a failure because of past mistakes. You may have a less than satisfactory family life or marriage, despite the absence of abuse. A loss that you think is resolved really is not, and it keeps bothering you with feelings of guilt, bereavement, and emptiness that you repress. Most likely, you repress the painful events or thoughts that give rise to your suffering.

It is a sad truth that if you have any unresolved issues in your life, they will not simply go away on their own.

They will sit in the subconscious part of your mind, manifesting in a myriad of ways. These ways include depression and anxiety, relationship problems, substance abuse, and other bad habits or patterns that interfere with your joy. They will bother you, while remaining hidden, until you finally resolve them. You will never be completely happy or at peace when you have some unresolved issue batting around in the darkness of your subconscious mind. It can be incredibly hard to face the things that hurt you in order to address them, but you have to if you want them to stop manifesting in your life.

Whatever sits at the core of your depression and anxiety needs to be brought to the light and resolved. Only once you find what is bothering you and address it, will you be able to move forward with your life. Addressing the root of your suffering is the first and most important part of healing. You simply cannot avoid this step. It is best to start on it now, and stop putting it off, no matter how much you want to. Aren't you tired of suffering? Aren't you tired of dealing with the horrific, disappointing, limiting, and painful effects that your mental problem has on your life? I know that I was by the time that I made a true commitment to healing and started working to get to the bottom of why I was sick.

But how can you possibly go about dredging up hidden things that you have become an expert at repressing? How can you stop the habit of lying to yourself and dismissing what is truly bothering you? How can you be sure that you find your true core issues, and that you truly resolve them?

Reaching the Bottom of the Issue

People's minds are like onions. There are many, many layers. As you begin to heal, start exploring each layer. Once you resolve the issues at one layer, you will be able to go deeper and address the next layer. It may take a while, but eventually you will reach the very core that lies at the epicenter of all of your pain and suffering. You will have removed all of the layers, all of the distracting issues and lies and repression mechanisms that you have used to bury the true cause of your pain. Then you will be able to address the final, core issue. You will also have the skills and strength to perform this kind of healing because you have developed them while dealing with the many previous layers of your conscious.

Let's start with the first layer. Then keep working on it. Therapy may help you, but the methods that I am about to share with you will help as well. Even if you use a therapist, he or she can only help you so much. Really, you are doing all of the work yourself either way. A therapist can only guide you, but he or she cannot do any of the work for you. This is your endeavor and you do have to do it alone. No one else can do the work for you, ever. Only you can reach that kind of depth in your own mind and only you can facilitate true healing. Be prepared to take on this journey alone, but feel free to set up supports who can guide you and hold you as you confront the pain that is troubling you so deeply.

Causes of Core Emotional Issues

There are two common causes of core emotional issues. The first is trauma, and the second is schemas, or self-beliefs. Work on identifying the things that lie at the very epicenter, or bottom, of your depression and anxiety.

Traumatic Events

A majority of your emotional wounds started forming in childhood. Events over the years have only added to the depth and pain of these wounds. A lot of your depression and anxiety can be traced back to events and traumas that hurt you as a child. These events may not seem like much on paper, but for some reason they really hurt you, so you should take them seriously. Sometimes, a death that happened when you were little does not cause you any pain, but if you really think about it, the confusion and grief that you felt over the loss and the way that your family dynamic changed following the loss can indicate that you did experience some emotional trauma over the death. You may not realize how much things hurt you as a child anymore, but there are certain childhood events that you can pinpoint that changed everything. Why did they change everything and how did you like that change? If they changed things in a bad way for you, and led to future struggles, then you can blame them for traumatizing you and contributing to your depression and anxiety now as an adult.

You can start getting to the bottom of your issues, or peeling away layers of the onion, by asking yourself questions. When you start to get upset by an event, ask yourself, "Why does this upset me so much? Did something like this happen to me in my childhood?"

Start dredging up the painful childhood memories that hurt you so badly. Allow yourself to really feel the hurt that you have buried. It will be painful, but allowing yourself to feel, allows you to let the feelings go. Now, imagine yourself as a child again. Imagine yourself apologizing to your child self for how badly you feel. Tell your child self that it will all be OK. Even imagine giving your child self a hug. This will help you dissipate the emotions and soothe the childhood hurt that dwells within you.

Another trick is to imagine the bad events or traumatic moments from your childhood. Really picture them vividly and clearly. Now take a snapshot, or freeze frame, of this event. Put a frame around it. Turn the picture black and white. Make it smaller and smaller and smaller until it is just a speck that you cannot see any details in. Do this every time you think about this bad event. This visualization helps you remove yourself from the event emotionally, so that you can analyze it and get over it without as much pain.

You can peel back another layer in your mind by analyzing your internal voice. Does the little voice in your head that criticizes you sound suspiciously like someone you know, such as your mother or father?

Then your mother or father probably criticized you too much, causing you to develop an internal overly critical voice. This voice may also be inspired from someone emotionally abusive that you may have known after childhood. An abusive ex, friend, teacher, or any other individual who spoke to you cruelly may have crippled your self-esteem as an adult. You may not realize that you were abused, but you were, and this manifests as your depression and anxiety because you have low self-esteem lying at the core of your issues. This voice is very successful at keeping you down and keeping your self-esteem very low. You need to work on changing this voice into something more positive.

When this voice from hell pops up in your head, practice making it sound like a cartoon voice. Chase away negative thoughts and self-talk with more positive thoughts and a kinder inner voice. Eventually, you will get into the habit of speaking to yourself nicely, rather than using the critical voice of a past abuser.

Are there any events that repeatedly pop into your head? Are there any unpleasant memories that you obsess over? Even if you no longer feel an obvious emotional response to these memories, they can still bring you down. Thinking about something a lot means that it is really bothering you in your subconscious – enough to slip into your conscious repeatedly. Think more about whatever memory you obsess over and try to find what bothers you about it. Try to think if it reminds you of an earlier memory, one that needs to be brought up and resolved. Also, let yourself truly feel the emotions that rise up in response to this memory. Don't repress them. Truly feeling this memory out will help you work through it.

Schemas

Abuse, rejection, and even past failures in business, school, or romance can cause you crippling internal wounds because they make you believe horrible things about yourself. They make you develop self-beliefs, also known as schemas, which chip away at your self-esteem and contribute to your bad feelings over years. A negative schema can lie at the bottom of your depression, or it may at least make up one of the layers of your illness.

You should question your self-beliefs, or schemas. Ask yourself, "What do I really think about myself? What thought first pops into my head when something good happens to me? Is it negative? Do I believe that I will mess things up, or that I don't deserve the good things that happen to me?" Usually, that initial thought that pops into your head indicates your schemas. More often than not, these schemas are negative.

Then, when you identify all of the horrible things that you believe about yourself, try to find evidence that these beliefs are not true. Essentially work on proving to yourself that your schemas are not true. Sadly, the human brain loves its schemas. It will cling to them fiercely. It will use every possible life situation as proof that your schemas are true. By now, your schemas are probably deeply rooted within you. You have to work to identify these schemas and uproot them. Don't let them bother you anymore. They are not true and you need to convince yourself of that fact.

Also change how you think about rejection and failure. Rejection is someone else's loss, not yours. People reject you because of their own issues, not because you are flawed or worthless as a person. Failure is a learning experience that has shaped you into the strong person that you are today and that has taught you many essential lessons. You will do better next time if you use past failures as lessons; don't believe that you don't get anything and that you are destined to fail at everything in life just because you failed at one thing or even many things in the past. These more positive beliefs will help you move past the rejections and failures that have added to your low self-esteem and keep bothering you in your subconscious.

Seven Questions

Try asking yourself a series of seven questions whenever you run into a problem. These questions will help you get to the bottom of the problem. Say you are depressed. You can ask seven questions to peel away layers of your metaphorical onion until you reach the very bottom:

Why am I so depressed?

Why do I have no energy?

Why do I hate myself? (List the things you hate about yourself that contribute to your low feeling.)

Why do I feel bad whenever I hang out with this particular person?

What happened just before my depressive episode?

Did this event remind me of anything from my past?

How can I feel better?

Understand the Hurt is Made up

All of the hurt that deepens your inner wounds is actually made up. You feel hurt because you misinterpreted a situation wrongly, for instance. Probably someone criticized you as a child, so now you think the worst about yourself and you reinforce that belief by noticing it when other people tend to criticize you or reject you. You think that the criticism spoke onto you as a child is true, so you believe it about yourself and you think that this flaw within yourself is responsible for all of your social problems. Now, you project this imagined flaw onto everything. Perhaps you have a friend who has drifted away from you. You don't know the real reason why, but you assume that it has to do with all of the flaws that you believe about yourself, because someone planted those flaws in your head.

Another example is if you feel that you are overweight. As a child, you may have been teased about being fat. Whether you really are fat or not, this weight problem has become a deep insecurity for you. You assume that everyone notices it and fixates on it as much as you do. Therefore, when a person rejects you romantically, you automatically assume that your weight is the reason why. You become hurt and you hate your body. You may even develop an eating disorder.

Most of the things that hurt you so deeply are really just imagined. You think that something is true, and you blow it up in your mind and project it onto everything in life. But has it ever occurred to you that maybe this belief is not true? Or that even if you do have a certain flaw, there are other reasons that people reject you, including reasons that really have nothing to do with you? A lot of the pain that you feel is probably unnecessary. So realizing what pain is unnecessary can aid you in getting over certain wounds and healing yourself. You need to embrace yourself and let go of the hurtful beliefs that you keep holding onto that bring you down and trigger your depression.

Make a List

Another great way to find your core hurt is to make a list of the things that typically really upset you. What events in life make you fly off the handle in rage, or make you question your goodness and worth as a human being? What events can make you fall into a severely depressed mood for a while or even a long time? What types of events stand out in your mind as repeatedly triggering your hurt? Are there any events that are rather commonplace, but cause you great emotional upset and turmoil? Any sort of romantic rejection might be one of these events, or not being invited to parties and outings with friends might be another. The slightest criticism or being overlooked at your job could be commonplace things that happen to everyone, yet these little events are enough to make you want to hurt yourself or drink yourself into a coma.

These events that hurt you so badly are things that activate your trigger. They somehow remind you of an event or schema that lies at the bottom of your consciousness, making you feel more upset than most people would in the same situation. Take a romantic rejection for instance. Romantic rejection hurts everyone, but it is a fairly commonplace occurrence. Lots of people get rejected. Often, the recipients of rejection are hurt, but they are able to eventually repair their self-esteem and move on. You, on the other hand, may get overly upset each time you are rejected. You may reach the point where you don't even try to date because rejection hurts you too much and you are sure that you will always be rejected. You ignore the many times that you were actually not rejected. This is because you came to believe that you were not good enough as a child, thanks to repeated barbs and critical comments from your emotionally abusive parents. Rejection hits your trigger because it seems to prove what your parents always told you. You get so hurt because rejection seems to tell you what you secretly believe, but don't want to be true.

You get upset about things that remind you of what you believe about yourself, but resist believing. It is very painful to confront these beliefs. But you need to. You need to tell yourself and even show yourself that your negative schemas are not true. Use things that upset you to identify negative schemas, and then address them.

Keep a Journal

As you go through this healing process, start keeping a detailed journal. Write in it every day and document your progress and your struggles. Write down things that bother you and analyze them.

A journal will help you keep everything straight. It will help you prevent forgetting important revelations or milestones. As you pass milestones in healing, you can congratulate yourself and give yourself a much-needed reward, such as a trip or spa day. Revisiting old entries can help you realize things that you have forgotten, and it can help you recognize patterns.

Patterns are especially important to watch out for. If some sort of event or issue keeps popping up in the pages of your journal, then it can indicate something deeper that you need to address. It could help you identify a trigger, which relates to a negative schema or horrible childhood memory.

You can also show your journal to your counselor if you choose to use counseling. He or she can use your journal as a means to see into your head and understand you better. He or she can point out things that you are missing or that you need to explore in more depth in your healing process. Otherwise, if you are not in counseling, reread your journal entries every now and then to help yourself see things more clearly and to explore things that you may need to revisit in more detail.

When you are finished with a journal, you can save it to review later. Or you can burn it. Burning your journal and its documentation of your struggles can be a symbolic demonstration of release. It can help you mentally let go of the struggles and bad memories and bitter emotions that are scrawled on the journal pages.

Chapter 13
Emotional Relief

Being mindful of your thought process is key to anxiety recovery. Here are some tips you can use to guide you through this process.

Self-control of emotions

Anxiety overcomers have mastered the art of controlling their thoughts and calming their minds. Some methods work better for some than others, as we are all different. One method is to control your breathing by focusing on it. Breathe in as you count to three and breathe out as you count to five. Think only about your breathing and counting. This forces your thoughts off of any negative situations, and onto just your breathing, with no other goal other than to control your mind.

Another method is to be as focused on the present time as you possibly can. As your grandmother may have said, "No sense in crying over spilled milk." There is absolutely nothing you can do about it or anything in your past. Worrying over matters that you cannot change is a primary stressor that can and should be avoided. If you have had a rough day or a rough month, bring yourself to the present. Don't be dismayed about anything that has happened in the past, or anything that might happen in the future. If you do this, you are training your brain to get ready for it, and it starts to build harmful neural networks to accommodate the negative activity to come. Think about your life right now, right here. Is there anything about your present condition that is favorable? Is there anything that you can be thankful for? Did you have food to eat today? Is there gas in your car? Can you walk and talk and see? There is someone out there less fortunate than you right now that is undergoing more dire circumstances than you. Take accurate stock of this hour, this minute. Analyze your thoughts right now. Are they helpful or positive? Try to appreciate the little things, like a flower, an orange, a smile. Go outside and feel the sunshine on your face. Look at your ten fingers and be thankful for them. Learn to see good in the little things, starting off even for a few minutes a day. Try to make that a habit, and you'll end up having a good day, even in the worst surroundings.

Still, another method is the self-talk. Science has proven that saying the right words to yourself shapes your senses and sends signals to your brain. Many of us unconsciously talk ourselves down, saying, "Stupid!" or another sarcastic remark, not realizing that your brain will make the necessary changes to accommodate your words. We need to use this for our benefit, not a detriment. Start looking in the mirror and telling yourself that "I am healthy and whole and healed, and I will have a calm, worry-free day. I am medically healthy and safe. This is only my body's fight or flight response, and nothing more. I am okay." It's important to use the word "I". These self-affirmations will affect you by triggering the circuitry of your brain that is responsible for reward or pleasure. When this is triggered, the flight-or-flight reactivity is overridden and you regain balance in your thought process. Let your self-affirmations focus on positive things that are happening right now in the present or positive goals you hope to experience in the future.

Another powerful method is to lightly analyze and distance yourself from your worries. For example, if you see your coworkers whispering in the break room and they get quiet when you walk in, you may immediately imagine that they're talking negatively about you. Change the scenario in your mind. It's not always about you. Imagine that they were talking about another issue that would anyone find out they'd be embarrassed about. Distance yourself from it and move on. Suppose your boss called your coworker in the office and shut the door. Don't imagine that your coworker is lying about you and you're about to be fired. Change the scenario. Maybe they're planning a birthday luncheon for someone else that is to be kept confidential. Get out of the habit of assuming that everyone is out to get you.

Stop looking for things to be offended by. It's not always about you! Maybe that person didn't see you and that's why they didn't hold open the elevator door for you. Give the person the benefit of the doubt. You aren't perfect, so don't expect anyone else to be. And if someone happens to do or say something inconsiderate or is intentionally obnoxious, make a conscious decision to let it go. Chalk it up to them having a really bad situation at home, or other circumstance that you'll never know about. Allow them to be the people they are, but distance your reactions. Now I'm not saying to let people walk all over you, but life is too short to have a mental and physical reaction to every possible negative outcome at every point of your day. As Charles Swindoll quoted, "I am convinced that life is 10% what happens to me and 90% of how I react to it."

Commanding control of your thoughts may take a while to completely master, especially if you've been negatively programmed for years and years. When your mind drifts to any thought that can make you anxious and worried, make your thoughts drift back to the present moment. The more you practice doing that, the easier it becomes, just like exercise. Distract your senses. This is a very powerful stress buster. Don't believe it? Try this exercise: In your mind, start reciting the alphabet. "A, B, C..." When you're halfway through, at the same time, and out loud, start counting down from 10. "10, 9, 8..." What happened? You know the alphabet by rote, and could say it backward and forwards if prompted, but when you were forced to focus on speaking the numbers, your internal thoughts about the alphabet were distracted. Your thoughts jumped to the numerical count down. You unconsciously distracted your thoughts of one process with the thoughts of another. Do the same when anxiety or panic starts to rear its ugly head.

You don't have to think of alphabets or speak numbers. Distract on purpose. Think of something pleasant, a beautiful flower, or a wonderful vacation you had in the past, or the smell of just-baked bread. Here's another exercise: Right now, think of a sweet, juicy lemon. "Feel" it in your hand. Imagine taking a small slice and putting it in your mouth. Didn't your face pucker? Didn't your saliva increase? That's because your brain was getting your body ready to eat the lemon. Use this technique consciously and train your brain to get your body ready to calm itself.

Schedule more of what makes you the happiest and peaceful, as long as it's healthy. Take a long bubble bath with aromatic candles. Try a new recipe, take a walk, get a dog, schedule a massage, play an instrument, learn scrapbooking, or read a nonsensical book. Actually, schedule these self-care events in your planner, just as if you were scheduling a meeting or a doctor appointment, or an oil change. Isn't your mental health worth it? If you've been overloaded and calendar-filled for years, you may not even know what makes you happy or peaceful. If this is the case, take a week and journal, and make a point to consciously recognize and jot down when you are the most relaxed, and what that environment consists of. Think of what you would do if money or time constraints weren't an issue. Then figure out how to create that environment responsibly. If you love to dance, join a dance class. If you love sunning on the beach that's not financially practical right now, find a quiet spot and a comfy couch, play beach music with the sounds of waves, close your eyes and imagine that you are there, even if only for ten minutes. Plan a free weekend and design a "staycay". Pretend that you and your family are tourists on vacation and do the things real tourists would do if they traveled to your city. Enjoy yourself, and don't feel an ounce of guilt about it! These activities don't have to be grandiose or monumental. In fact, studies have shown that if you schedule one activity every day that makes you feel happy or satisfied, the effects last longer and are far-reaching.

Laugh! Laughter relieves stress, improves circulation, relaxes your muscles, and decreases your blood pressure and heart rate, and has proven to be more beneficial than even music therapy. When you laugh, your body also produces chemicals that relieve pain naturally. The levels of stress hormones like cortisol are reduced, and the reward center of the brain activates the release of dopamine. Laughter lightens your mood, decreases anxiety and depression, spurs collaboration and creativity at the office, burns calories, and even increases the production of good (HDL) cholesterol. When you can get to the point of laughing at your situations, the stress somehow starts to fade away. You can actually practice laughing. Start out with "Ha-Ha". Keep it going. What starts out as forced can shift to natural and spontaneous. There are even classes that practice laughter. Try to make it a normal part of your day, being careful to not laugh at others. Consciously turn your frown into a smile, and your body will physically respond, even if the smile is forced. A good belly laugh yields some of the same changes to your body as to when you exercise, even if the changes last only for the duration of the laughter. If you find it difficult to do this on your own, find a laughing class in your area. Yes, there are indeed laugh classes. If there are none where you live, find online classes or videos and have fun! One such video is the "iPhone laughing commercial" on YouTube. Look it up, and laugh away!

Therapy

One of the best therapeutic helps with overcoming anxiety is understanding that that is what you are suffering from. It sounds simplistic, but once you get a medical clearance and know that there are no major health issues that you're dealing with, and that you aren't having a heart attack, and that you are not losing your mind, the healing begins.

Sometimes though, the issue has been so severe in the past, that it may be wise to get professional help to help you through the process. Therapy may not work as fast as prescribed medicines, but it can be just as or more effective as a treatment. In most instances, combining medicine and therapy is the best course of action. If needed get your primary doctor to recommend a therapist or go to your local college or university and review their counseling services. Get a full physical and rule out any and all medical conditions. Once this is obtained, and the person realizes that their mind is the main culprit, then the real work can begin. Psychoanalysis helps you to see the automatic triggers in your life. It may help you see the truth.

Anti-anxiety therapy should include behavioral exercises and training to moderate response to stimuli. This is called CBT, or cognitive behavioral therapy. Behavioral techniques and cognitive therapy help you behave differently by changing your usual thought patterns, beliefs, and behavior. The effectiveness of CBT alone varies from study to study. Some report that it is as effective, or more effective, than medication alone, and that it has long-term benefits that you can self-apply at any time in the future. Others report that without the added benefit of anti-anxiety medications, CBT is effective only half of the time. The actual effectiveness depends on the level of disorder, the quality of the therapist, and your willingness to ungrudgingly participate in the sometimes rudimentary applications.

A CBT therapist relies on case formulation to determine the cause of the anxiety. Learning about the clients' predisposing factors will shed light on what influencers, like personality, genetics, or major life events, contributed to the development of a problem-oriented existence. After reviewing these predispositions, the therapist will work with the client to identify what specific triggers or events led to the anxiety first manifesting. Next, together the therapist and client pinpoint any current factors that perpetuate, or reinforce, the anxiety. Finally, the therapist helps identify what existing positive factors there are in the clients' life that, if properly reinforced and guided, could help them overcome anxiety, such as a supporting family, or grit and determination, or a strong desire to want to change.

One CBT technique is to try to eliminate cognitive distortions that anxiety sufferers often exhibit. These are thoughts that are incorrect or not completely correct. These untruths or partial untruths strengthen the very negative emotions they try to avoid. CBT therapists try to help sufferers identify these issues in themselves. For example, when a person jumps to conclusions, they are sure that something has happened or will happen even without any evidence to support that conclusion. Another example is the glass half full syndrome. Two people can analyze the exact same situation and come to two opposite conclusions – positive or negative – based upon their own internal disposition. Many with anxiety don't realize that they often overestimate the likelihood and the extent of undesirable outcomes. With this realization comes the unraveling of the distortion. Once you figure out what happened that made you start feeling this way, you can begin to challenge it.

Another CBT technique that therapists recommend is journaling. Start journaling and analyze your own thinking. Jot down when you feel the most anxious, and the actual thoughts that are making you feel more and more anxious. Analyze what you are thinking and experiencing during these times. Write down the time of day, and your location when the anxiety manifested. Analyze on a scale of one to ten whether or not you believe the thoughts, and from one to ten analyze the intensity of the emotions brought about by these thoughts. Replace those thoughts with logical thoughts based upon your clean bill of health. Say positive affirmations to yourself that in reality, all is well and you will be okay. Write down these alternative thoughts and affirmations. When an issue that is small suddenly feels all-consuming, remember that it is not the end of the world. Don't identify yourself with this one small situation. Step back, take a breath and notice something beautiful. Finally, jot down the result of the exercise, and if you were successful in confronting the anxiety-laden thought. Write if the alternative thought or affirmation that you wrote down convinced you and if the force of the emotions diminished. Share your journaling findings with your therapist.

Journaling has a number of benefits, such as organizing your thoughts. Once you jot them down on paper, you're free to leave them for a while and get back to them later. The writing process forces you to take the chaos out of your mind and organize them on paper. This practice calms the mind, and if done regularly, is a powerful instrument for healing. It will be important that you designate only a set time to review these notes, so you won't start to rehash them.

A third CBT technique is exposure. This therapy encourages people to master their fears, one at a time, by constant exposure to it. This is most helpful for sufferers of OCD. They expose themselves to the triggers of their compulsive behaviors and try to not exhibit the behavior. This in combination with journaling is helpful to identify how you feel when going through these exercises.

Scripting is a CBT technique that seems logical but is effective. When those with anxiety actually identify the worst possible scenarios of what they most fear, they can recognize that even if this does happen, they'll still be able to manage it. "What if" scenarios may help you rationally work through how to manage if things do go as wrong as they think. It also helps you to recognize the myriad of ways that things could possibly go right. Either way, thinking through the possibilities does seem to help override illogical predictions of doom and destruction.

Another CBT technique that helps you to face what seems to be absolutely overwhelming, is to identify the steps it will take to get to the end desired result. If there is a major goal or pending event that will require a major effort, it can paralyze the anxiety sufferer into doing nothing at all. One way to end this cycle is to not focus on the entire end goal but on bite-sized, manageable steps. Dividing the steps into smaller, conquerable tasks, makes a mountain look more like a series of molehills. You don't need to know all of the required steps of the project, only the first few steps. Aiming for the completion of the first small steps lessens the insurmountable pressure to handle everything at once.

Scheduling activities to put an end to the isolation normally associated with anxiety and depression is actually a CBT technique as well. These activities should be ones that you enjoy, and that you've identified as when you feel your best, like taking a walk. You can also schedule activities to help combat procrastination. If there is something you've been avoiding, clear your schedule on a particular day and schedule it in. The discipline of following a schedule, and the successful accomplishment of scheduled daily activities, leads to more self-confidence. In addition, the isolation is managed, if not reversed.

The imagery exposure CBT technique helps you to analyze your thoughts about a recent event that formed an intense negative emotion. When we perceive that something happened that is hurtful, such as a mean comment or expression, we tend to mull it over in our minds, basically reliving the experience over and over again. This imagery, guided by a therapist, still has you visualize the event but encourages you to identify the specific thoughts and emotions you experienced, and the impulses you felt inclined to act upon, like crying or shouting. It is believed that when you repeatedly visualize the event and experience the same urges and emotions, that the power of the emotional trigger behind it is eliminated. PTSD sufferers require significantly more intense therapeutic exposure protocols, some of which involve actually assisting the person to re-live the event in a controlled environment. The nightmare is discussed in such a detail that a similar feeling or emotion arises. The therapist works to create a new image that leads to a more desired emotive response. The more often this occurs, the more successful the recovery. Group sharing with others who have experienced the same trauma is also a positive treatment method. The earlier PTSD is treated, the more successful the treatment.

Cognitive restructuring is a CBT therapeutic method that uses Socratic questioning. It is called Socratic questioning because the philosopher Socrates developed this educational method and utilized it when teaching. This method attempts to encourage you to figure out the answers to your own questions. It motivates you to think for yourself and to dig deep and find the answers you often seek. When applied to cognitive restructuring, this method forces you to challenge and alter illogical thoughts.

Using this Socratic methodology, therapists get their patients to express what they are thinking or one particular thought that may be causing apprehension or uneasiness. Once that is identified, a discussion is started about the facts that either contradict or support the thought. What are the facts in this situation? Not what your feelings are about it, but the facts. Once these facts are identified, a conversation begins to analyze, based upon the facts, if the original thought was the truth, or was it emotion or opinion. Questions are asked that assist in this process, and to identify from where or from whom the thought originated, and if the situation or thought was based upon misinterpreted evidence or unconfirmed expectations. The therapist guides the patient to honestly express if the truth was inflated and if the thought was entertained merely out of habit, regardless of the truth. Lastly, the therapist helps you identify whether the situation is likely or unlikely, and to determine all of the possible scenarios. Questions of this Socratic methodology help you to deeply examine the thoughts that cause so much angst and help you evaluate your thought process. If you have thoughts that are just not true or are exaggerated, this process helps you to identify and neutralize them.

Support Groups

Reach out to others who have already conquered anxiety (many out there). It is very helpful to realize that you're not the only one with these issues. Just talking about it with someone who understands is quite a stress reliever. If you can't find someone, ask your doctor to recommend an anxiety support group. It's important to feel connected, as anxiety usually leads to isolation. Talking over your experiences is a great healing process. That alone relieves the stress of thinking that you're the only one experiencing this. One added benefit of an anxiety support group is that, since they've all experienced it, you can get unbiased and honest opinions about how the group members see you and how they think of you. Often, you'll find that the image you have about yourself is distorted, inaccurate, or untrue. These types of interactions are helpful, and will also help you get over the fear of unpleasant social situation.

Conclusion

Anxiety can be a crippling disorder that leaks into all aspects of a person's life. It can impact their relationships or performance at school or work, alter a person's general happiness, and cause a person to feel isolated from the world around them, and even lead to thoughts of suicide. This is why it is vital to put in the work to cure the disorder.

Feeling worried over a stressful situation is common. A person that has recently been unemployed will most likely feel particularly tense at the beginning of the month when they are forced into paying all of their bills. They may lose sleep over the situation and struggle to function until it is solved, but if their anxiety goes away when the situation is cured then they have simply had a normal reaction to a stressful situation. If, once the unemployed person finds work but is still haunted by the thought that they may be fired once more, then it becomes a different problem. Their worry has become chronic and is taking over their life. Perhaps they no longer want to go out with friends because they're frightened that they will lose their job and so feel the need to save their money. Maybe they insist on living so humbly that it becomes ridiculous (only spending money on the absolute necessities in life) and causing their relationships around them to suffer.

When it becomes a chronic condition that is harming your quality of life, it is necessary to seek help. The different branches of anxiety need to be treated individually, and the roots of the anxiety must be identified in order to move on from it. A person suffering from a panic disorder will benefit most from diagnosing the specific cause of their fear before they will benefit from following the steps to help alleviate depression and anxiety. A person suffering from severe shyness may suffer the same symptoms as a person with Generalized Anxiety Disorder, but needs to still address the reasons for their shyness before they can follow those steps also. Therefore, it is necessary to respect the disorder for exactly what it is.

Most children fear the dark and are usually gently transitioned from sleeping with the light on, to a nightlight, to sleeping without any light on. If the fear has stuck with a person into adulthood and now haunts them at night (to the extent that they sleep with all the lights on in their room), then it has become a chronic fear. The person has to address the reasons behind the fear (e.g., feeling vulnerable without a sense of sight) in order to fully move on from the situation.

Avoidance or aversion will never help treat a person with fears that they must encounter in their lives. Take a person who is terrified of flying but offered a job in a city far from their hometown (and friends and family). Suddenly, that person is conflicted with the decision to either not take the job due to their crippling fear, even though the job offers more money and a better lifestyle than the one that they are currently in, or take the job but be forced into the torment of riding on an airplane. Choosing to do something that forces you to face your fears is brave, and if the person never gets on the plane then they

will be both haunted by the fact that their fear will only mount (news stories involving planes never end well; if this is the only information a person has on flying it is obvious why they would struggle with the idea) and have missed out on a great opportunity over something that could have been easily cured.

Our senses are one of the most helpful things in helping us stay present and in the moment, because they are always in action (even if we don't always pay attention to them). A person that experienced assault in their life may not remember all the senses they felt at the moment the trauma was happening, until later on when the senses that they felt at that time become their triggers. Suddenly, a person is left unable to function when someone touches their hair or is wearing a certain type of perfume or cologne. Something as simple as a chill in the air could be enough to cause a person to feel terror when they least expect it. Although the fact that these cues exist may not be changed, the ability to combat them can be learned. Through identifying the specific steps that occur right before a panic attack, you will be able to remain in control of your body. One of the most terrifying parts of panic attacks, as already stated, is that when they occur the sufferer often feels as though they are dying. This thought, combined with the memories of a past trauma, can cripple a person with fear. The panic attack itself can be traumatic, but the steps stated above can aid in combating it. Something as small as having hand lotion in your pocket or handbag at all times will make a huge difference (extra points if it's lavender scented!).

Unfortunately, it is necessary to face your fears rather than avoid them. A good way of doing this is by facing them in short increments of time. For example, if you're frightened of spiders, begin by setting yourself the goal of looking at a picture of one for a few seconds each day for a week. When that week is over, make yourself look at pictures for a few more seconds each day. Build yourself up to eventually going to the reptile house at a zoo and seeing a tarantula face-to-face.

It is important to set yourself goals. If you're looking to overcome a fear, then follow the steps above but give yourself a timeline. For example, give yourself three weeks before you physically see a spider, but no longer than that or you will have not pushed yourself hard enough. Perhaps your goal is to overcome your shyness; an attainable way of doing that is to simply speak to a new person each day.

Every day, set yourself the goal of asking a person how their day is going. It is simpler than you think, particularly in America. This is because everywhere you go there are people working in stores and restaurants that are paid to smile at you and ask you how you're doing. Therefore, make it a goal that every time you are at the supermarket you ask the cashier how their day is going, or if you order a drink at a bar begin by simply greeting the bartender, or even if you pass a neighbor that you've felt too hesitant to greet before, just give them a smile. Not only will your comfort level with speaking to new people grow, but you could also make new friends from it.

If you are seriously looking to pull yourself out of your comfort zone in order to fight your shyness, theater can be an amazing help. Most places have a community theater and would be very receptive to somebody using it as a platform to overcome their shyness (as discussed with the example of Matt taking theater as a way to break away from his inability to speak to people). Improvisation groups can also be a fun way to break out of your shell; who knows, maybe you'll discover how funny you really are!

Depression and anxiety are two disorders that often intertwine. Anxiety combined with depression worsens it and can make it much more of a struggle to live with. Both disorders can leave a person feeling isolated from those around them, and each alone has a risk of suicidal thoughts so together they increase it dramatically. Lifestyle changes are essential to battling these forces.

Diet is a huge component of depression and anxiety, and a good place to begin is by cutting out as many processed foods as possible. If you are a person that would feel deprived by never having a slice of pizza again (as arguably many would), then it is reasonable to plan a night a week where you have a "cheat" meal. Make sure though that the rest of your meals are well-rounded with complex carbohydrates, fruits and vegetables, and protein. There is an emphasis on fish, which contain Omega-3 fatty acids, as they have been proven to have a positive effect on a person suffering from depression. If there are nutrients that you are unable to consume due to dietary regulations (because of allergies, for example), then consulting with your doctor will help you figure out how to round out your diet in a way that's most beneficial to you.

Exercise is another proven way of combating anxiety and depression. It does not have to be complex — nobody is telling you to prepare for a triathlon (although it would be an amazing goal to set yourself!). Instead, it is about doing the activity that you enjoy. If you enjoy walking, then a daily thirty minute walk will have a huge impact on your overall health, as well as leaving you feeling relaxed. Yoga is a great way to improve your deep breathing and make you feel more connected to your body. This is particularly useful to a person that suffers from panic attacks, as gaining control of your breathing is a huge step in fighting panic attacks.

Remember that everything that goes into fighting anxiety and depression intertwines. Exercise will help you form a better sleep cycle, and by incorporating it in your daily routine you are likely to not have time for napping (which throws your body out of synch). Make sure that you don't exceed the amount of sleep you are supposed to get in an evening. For a person suffering from severe depression, monitoring your sleep can be difficult, but this is why we have discussed making sure you set yourself goals and still take on responsibility. Plan your exercise for the morning before work, or if you control your shifts, then ask your boss to begin earlier in the day. If you are still a student, take thirty minutes before class to read over your notes; that way you will be out of bed earlier but also better prepared for class, which will make you feel more in control of the situation (and in turn less anxious).

The discomfort that you may feel at the thought of taking these steps to a better life is guaranteed to be less than the discomfort you will feel if you continue to live a life filled with depression, anxiety, panic attacks, fear, and severe shyness. The proven techniques we have discussed will help you take control and live a happier life than ever before.

Printed in Great Britain
by Amazon